SNIPER
ON THE
EASTERN FRONT

SNIPER
ON THE
EASTERN FRONT

THE MEMOIRS OF SEPP ALLERBERGER
KNIGHTS CROSS

EDITED BY
Geoffrey Brooks

Pen & Sword
MILITARY

First published in Great Britain in 2005 by
Pen & Sword Military
an imprint of
Pen & Sword Books Ltd
47 Church Street
Barnsley
South Yorkshire
S70 2AS

ISBN 1 84415 317 7

Typeset by Kirsten Barber,
Leeds, West Yorkshire

I dedicate this book to my daughter,
Angie Valeria Brooks-Canepa

Contents

The route followed by Josef Sepp Allerberger
from the battle of Redkina Gap near
Voroshilovsk,
July 1943

USSR

R. Donetz

R. Dnieper

REDKINA GAP
First engagement
July 1943

Crossed on
16 Mar 1944

R. Bug

10 Apr 1944

NIKOPOL
Oct 1943–Feb 1944

BISTRITZ
May–Aug
1944

Battle at Bakalov
5 Apr 1944

RUMANIA

Black Sea

Author's Introduction

I am a German, born ten years after World War II. My generation grew up with slogans like "All Germans are Nazis", "All Germans are War Criminals" and "Being a German means to be the European underdog". As a seven-year-old boy, a French baker called me a "Boche" (pig) and would not sell me a croissant. I was nine when my school-class was forced to watch a two hour documentary during a visit to Auschwitz showing appalling SS cruelty to the prisoners. I was forty when a British visitor of the Imperial War Museum greeted me with 'Heil Hitler, Fritz' when he recognized I was German.

So it will be a delicate matter to publish outside Germany in English the story of a German World War II sniper.

It took me nearly fifteen years' negotiation with Mr Allerberger, the protagonist of this book, before he agreed to talk fully to me about his war service. After many long days of serious conversation we decided to tell his story like it really was. Our aim has been to give the reader a no-holes-barred insight into life – and death – on the Eastern Front rather than a variety of official war history.

The reader of this edition, translated by Geoffrey Brooks, which tells Allerberger's story in the first person, should be aware that my original book was in narrative form. We have discussed this at length as I prefer the way I did it. If English language readers accept this book, as we hope they will, we will seriously consider bringing out a further edition translated directly from my original work with more pictures. I would welcome your views through Pen and Sword Books.

Prologue

The end of the monumental battle of Stalingrad was for Hitler's beleaguered army the beginning of a two year withdrawal west. This protracted campaign on the Eastern Front will for ever symbolise the German soldier's fighting ability in the face of extreme adversity.

Inevitably much has been written, both factual and analytical, about this theatre of operations. Yet to find words to describe the level of human suffering, the daily struggle for survival against both the elements and the enemy, and the horror and the fear is well nigh impossible for those who were not there. Only those who were can adequately attempt to portray their experiences and emotions.

The man whose story is in this book was a sniper. It is important to understand from the outset the standing of this elite breed of soldier. To their own side they are admired and respected for their military skills, their ability to operate on their own, often behind enemy lines, and for their contribution which can be truly significant. To the enemy they are the lowest of the low, no better than cold-blooded murderers who strike indiscriminately without warning. If the sniper survives and, given the nature of their trade, the vast majority do not, they have to live with the knowledge that they have destroyed so many victims' lives. Not surprisingly nearly all will shut out their experiences as though they never happened. This explains why personal accounts are so rare and sought-after.

After fifty years one of the most skilled German snipers decided to break the silence and share his extraordinary experiences with his biographer during lengthy conversations. Naturally so long after those terrible events some memories are much sharper than others and it was necessary to connect these anecdotes into a cohesive whole. Often this involved filling gaps and painting in the background with the results of thorough research. Only in this way could the story be presented in a complete form.

One more problem confronted the biographer, which can be expressed through the saying, 'he who wins is right but he who loses is wrong'. So while Russian and Allied marksmen are honoured as heroes, German snipers are seen as evil assassins. Strangely this can even be the case in their own country.

What follows is the story of Sepp Allerberger. Before the war Sepp was a carpenter in a small village near Salzburg, but, like so many young men, he was thrown into the maelstrom of war. His unit, *Gebirgsjäger-Regiment 144* of the *3rd Gebirgs Division* was deployed on the Eastern Front. Sepp was among his fellows as the vast majority of the soldiers were from his alpine region and this no doubt accounted for their high morale and closeness, which they managed to maintain in spite of so many set-backs and hardships.

As the following account vividly describes, the withdrawal from Stalingrad was a supreme test for all those involved. After the annihilation of 6th Army, the *3rd Gibergs Division* somehow managed to escape encirclement and thereby avoid the fate of so many of their fellow countrymen. After a murderous winter fight in the Millerowo basin, which reduced Sepp's Regiment to a quarter of its established fighting strength, the Division broke out.

Over the following months, *Regiment 144* were able to make a firm stand near Woroschilowsk and were restored to full strength with new drafts and equipment. By comparison with the earlier battles they had experienced, Allerberger and his comrades-in-arms were initially confronted with only light opposition, rather than all-out assaults. There was one serious irritant, however, and that was the constant threat from Russian snipers. On the whole the marksmen's victims were the new, more inexperienced soldiers. The defending Germans found themselves almost helpless in the face of this constant threat. The snipers were hard to locate and, even when their positions were discovered, it took mortars and medium machine guns to dislodge of them and these were in all too short supply.

It became obvious to the Germans that they were in dire need of trained marksmen to take the fight to the enemy.

Chapter 1

Machine-Gunner at the Ukraine Front, September 1943

I was born in September 1924. Our home was in a small village on the Austrian side of the Bavarian Alps near Salzburg. On leaving school I was apprenticed to my father, a master carpenter who ran a small workshop with a couple of employees. Notices of eligibility for conscription into the German *Wehrmacht* were distributed to our village in the autumn of 1942. It was a red-letter day for everybody. We twelve heroes turned out in our Sunday best, the fire-brigade band played a rousing serenade, the *Bürgermeister* delivered a stirring speech mentioning the Fatherland and its struggle against world Bolshevism. Afterwards, girls of the *Bund Deutscher Mädchen* or BDM (The Girls' Hitler Youth) gave each of us a large posy to be worn in the hatband of our Tyrolean headgear or, if we were hatless, draped over the lapel and left shoulder of our jackets. Then we sat for a group photograph. None of us gave a thought to the possibility of our young lives being cut short in battle. When the war ended, only six of our group were still alive.

I was able to complete my joinery apprenticeship before my formal conscription into *Gebirgsjäger* Regiment 144 (G.J.R. 144) of 3.*Gebirgsdivision* (3.G.D.) in February 1943. The division recruited principally from the Bavarian Alps region. At Kufstein I passed a sham medical to be declared '*Kriegsverwendungsfähig*' – fit for the front – and after the usual entry formalities, received my uniform issue and reported ten days later to the infantry depot at Mittenwald, west of Berchtesgaden. When I completed training six months later I was a qualified sMG-gunner. Never once throughout the basic course did I ever hear the term 'sniper' as a tactical component in infantry warfare as waged either by ourselves or the Soviets, although mention was made of male and female Russian sharpshooters who tended to fire upon us from positions rearward

1

of the front line and who were the primary target for machine-gunners.

The training was hard and the discipline, though lacking the chicanery which had characterized it pre-war, allowed no time for innocent loafing. The new recruit had to be brought to the peak of physical fitness and weapons handling. Instructors with front experience were at pains to pass on their practical knowledge; they knew the risks for the newcomer to the front.

At the beginning of September 1943 I received my marching orders to join G.J.R. 144 in the southern sector of the Eastern Front near Voroshilovsk, a town in the Ukraine a few hundred kilometres north of the eastern end of the Sea of Azov. For the majority there was a last opportunity to take leave of their families with a three-day leave pass. My mother stroked her hand tenderly over my head: my father, a soldier in the Great War, hid his concern behind a stiff upper lip and great industry in his carpentry workshop. When I was about to board the bus for Mittenwald barracks, my mother burst into tears and my father hugged me, something he had never done before. Clearly restraining his emotions, he whispered: 'Take care, my boy. I wish from the bottom of my heart that you come home safely. But everything lies in God's hands.' As the bus drove away from the village, I waved back once and then stared ahead, otherwise for sure I would have cried myself.

Within days we were trundling across the endless Russian steppe for the Donetz Basin. Each cattle truck had a deep litter of straw and was part of a long train pulled by two locomotives and protected against enemy aircraft and partisans by 20mm flak quadruples in cupolas on two freight chassis. It was July in Russia, and baking hot.

The loss of 250,000 men with all their armament and equipment at Stalingrad at the beginning of 1943 had marked the turn of the tide for the *Wehrmacht*. On two consecutive evenings, 18 and 19 December 1942, *Feldmarschall* von Manstein had requested that Hitler allow the 6.Army to break out of the encirclement at Stalingrad, this being the only way to save the mass of the men. In this he had the vociferous support of Zeitzler, Chief of the General Staff, but Hitler turned down the suggestion. To retreat a step, anywhere, was against his military philosophy. The last hope was now *Feldmarschall* Paulus, as the diary entry of Hitler's Army adjutant, Major Gerhard Engel for 22 December 1942 makes clear:

2

FHQ Wehrwolf. Deepest depression here. Nearly everybody hoping that P. would take the risk and attempt to break out contrary to his orders. He would at least save the men, if at enormous loss in materials. Jodl spoke very seriously this evening, and one could see that he was banking on this independent decision.[1]

But Paulus was no Manstein, nor even a Jodl, and the 6.Army stayed at Stalingrad to rot. During the winter of 1942/43, G.J.R. 144 of 3.G.D. fought south of Stalingrad and narrowly escaped becoming involved in the encirclement. After murderous winter fighting at Millerov and breaking out to join the new front at Voroshilovsk, the regiment had been reduced to a quarter of its authorized strength. The regiment dug in and was reconstituted with men and equipment over the next six months. During this rest it was fortunate to be confronted by little more than nuisance raids, from which the odd skirmish resulted, the occasional artillery barrage and Russian sniper fire. The latter claimed its victims, particularly among new arrivals and the inexperienced. Most of the time the Germans were helpless against the sniper phenomenon due to the shortage of heavy weapons. It was a relatively rare occurrence that a sniper was located and engaged with medium infantry weapons such as mortars, MGs or the rare PAK anti-tank gun. The German side suffered from a total lack of snipers.

I belonged to a group making up the last personnel replacements bringing G.J.R. 144 to full strength. For three weeks, 3.G.D. had been watching with alarm as the Red Army, strengthened by supplies of new American weapons, was equipping for a new offensive in the Donetz Basin and the Ukraine, and so every new recruit arriving at Voroshilovsk was extremely welcome. Upon our arrival we had the 'fortune' to experience our baptism of fire immediately. Without having an opportunity to acclimatize, we were pitched into the extremely bitter and bloody fighting in the Redkina Gap a day after arriving. We had been dealt a bum hand from the bottom of the pack, and for the remainder of the war, 3.G.D. was used purely as infantry, always present at the hotspots of the fighting in the southern section of the Eastern Front. Our losses were enormous and in the final reckoning, exceeded by several times the authorized personnel strength.

The Donetz Basin, with its extensive coal-mines, was an important supplier of raw material. This ensured it was a focus of great interest to the opposing belligerents. The mines with their huge gallery systems had not been investigated and mopped-up during the German advance. Whole Soviet battle-groups lurked underground, allowing *Wehrmacht* units to pass overhead. Wherever they were in a position to do so, these Russian forces would appear suddenly as if from nowhere to attack the German line from behind. Such encounters developed into fearsome hand-to-hand engagements which often spilt back down into the galleries.

With great energy the Soviets had already breached the German line and were now attempting to widen the bridgehead. The 3.G.D. commander considered the situation to be so dangerous that he launched an immediate counter-attack without prior preparation or the regrouping of his forces. This succeeded, but amounted to a pyrrhic victory.

At first light on 18 July 1943 we *Jäger*[2] moved stealthily towards our forward trenches, tension and nervousness etched into hard facial features. Each man had his own method of overcoming his anxiety before each fresh engagement – chewing on a lump of black bread, smoking, urinating or evacuating frequently – while most of the new arrivals seemed to have a motor disorder and jerked from place to place. I watched it all with acute discomfort. My own condition was not good: my stomach rebelled at the thought of food and my limbs felt like jelly. In such a critical situation I realized what a godsend it was to have a veteran platoon commander long since baptized with 'the waters of the front'. Noticing my fear, he spoke to me in soothing tones: 'Just keep taking deep breaths, *Junge*, keep your mind on your MG and shoot just like you have been trained. Watch for my signals. I look after my boys and I will be there with you in the thick of it. So far I have brought my platoon out of every shemozzle, and I haven't lost a man yet.' His words, the truth of the latter sentence highly dubious, gave me strength to overcome my anxieties and stand firm in the face of whatever horrors my baptism of fire were to bring.

The first stage of our attack began at just before five with an artillery barrage. The idea seemed to be to plough the terrain in front of us in progressive stages. The earth was turned over with a succession of dull thuds, the explosion from each shell spraying large clumps of sod into the clear morning sky. As each salvo lengthened, I became aware of strange sickening screams amidst the roars of shells impacting and the whizzing sigh of metal splinters. We German

Jäger cowered in our trenches and awaited the order to advance. After about twenty minutes the artillery barrage fell away and an ominous silence fell, through which the terrible cries of the Russian wounded were clearly audible. The order came to attack. Suddenly all my nervousness disappeared.

The battle sucked us forward across the broken earth like a whirlwind. The Russian artillery opened fire. As I rose up from my trench the first shells began to explode in our ranks. I heard a whizzing, ripping noise nearby. My comrade immediately to the right, an eighteen-year-old from Berchtesgaden, had been hit. A splinter had ripped open his tunic and abdomen, allowing his intestines to pour free. After a second or so of disbelief he attempted to restore the steaming organs. I laid down my MG, thinking it my duty to help him. The NCO (non-commissioned officer) clapped my shoulder and shouted: 'Forward, attack! There's nothing more you can do for your friend, give the men covering fire!' The wounded youth had sunk to his knees, from where he fell face first in the churned earth: I retrieved the MG and scrambled forward, my mind empty of thought. The primeval instinct for survival had taken possession of me. Death, fear, anxiety had lost their meaning. Shoot, reload, move forward was the only Reality: seek cover, search for the enemy like an animal of prey. Within me a strange metamorphosis was taking place. The low-brow who had risen from the trench would, during the next few hours of violent battle, become an infantryman, better still a warrior in the original sense of the word. Fear, blood, death were the ingredients in an alchemy that intoxicated and drugged its participant: it marked the end of my personal innocence and swept away all visions and dreams of 'my future'; swept away my life. I was being forced to kill. Killing on the battlefield was to be my trade. Fate required of me that I should perfect it to mastery.

For a brief while we moved forward unmolested by enemy fire. Protected by the MGs on its flanks, our group crept warily through the bushy terrain. When firing commenced from a concealed position in the undergrowth about 20 metres away, a *Jäger* fell without a sound in the stream of bullets from a machine-pistol. I returned MG-fire without hesitation while the men threw themselves down. Once a salvo of stick-grenades had silenced the Russian fire, the *Jäger* snaked forward to the enemy hide, which was by now abandoned. Beyond the bushes lay the bodies of four dead Russians who had fallen just short of the entrance to the artfully concealed underground gallery. It had probably been their home for months. Fresh tracks led into the shaft. A mixture of curiosity and fascination drove the *Jäger* patrol, rifles cocked, ever deeper into the abysmal darkness. A few minutes after the ground had swallowed them, I heard the dull sound of shooting from within, and a brief while later the patrol tumbled out into the daylight, all of them white as a sheet, some retching, all visibly horrified. There was no time for questions, for just then a Russian company launched a fresh attack, and the whirlwind of the fire-fight tore us away with it. The bitter struggle continued until dusk fell at about ten, when our platoon retired to the forward trenches from where we had embarked upon our advance early that morning. The extent of the Russian resistance had been underestimated and we would have to repeat the whole procedure on the morrow. Both sides reorganized overnight allowing each other a few hours' rest.

The pause was also used to distribute ammunitions and rations, and bandage the walking wounded still able to fight. I considered it a minor miracle that I had spent the day without incurring a scratch, in contrast to many of my comrades. Squatting with a chunk of bread, a tin of sardines and a cigarette, we reviewed the events of the day in brief snatches of conversation. I asked about the occurrence in the underground gallery. In pithy sentences filled with undisguised disgust and horror, the two surviving *Jäger* told their story. It involved an event, irrational and incomprehensible such as often occurs in war, which gave us an insight into the type of enemy, the type of human beings (if you could call them such) that the political commissars were.

Gingerly feeling their way forward through the gloom, our patrol had progressed about 50 metres when they came to an ill-lit alcove around which wafted a bestial stink. They waited for their eyes to accustom to the darkness and then took it all in. In one corner cowered two Russian soldiers, youths who appeared to be about sixteen, huddled together for safety. In another corner were a number of ammunition boxes arranged to make a table which bore the remains of a dismembered human body. The cadaver had apparently been smoked over a fire for preservation and later use as rations. A third corner had been set aside for the usual ablutions and general waste, which now included putrefying body parts, bones and human organs rejected for consumption. Curious, a *Jäger* asked the two

6

trembling Russian survivors for an explanation. He was assisted by a *Jäger*-interpreter who happened to speak some Russian.

The two young Russians stated that during the Soviet retreat in August the previous year when German Panzers, rolling forward towards Maikop and the Russian oilfields, had overrun Voroshilovsk, thirty-five Russian soldiers had been left behind with strict instructions to occupy this gallery unnoticed for as long as possible, or until the Russian counter-offensive succeeded. As the months passed by, the supplies became exhausted. The group leader, a political commissar, had been charged with the strictest enforcement of the orders. When finally the men had mustered the courage to protest and demand a withdrawal from the gallery, the commissar had simply put down the little revolt by drawing his pistol and shooting two protesters in the head. Brandishing the weapon towards the survivors, he had ordered them to eviscerate the bodies and smoke the flesh over a fire. The livers, being edible fresh, were to be removed and divided into equal portions for immediate consumption. Over the next few weeks the smoked human flesh had supplemented their rations. The political officer had the support of his sergeant and two NCOs who kept the weapons under lock and key. Once the requirement arose for more meat, the commissar selected another victim and shot him. It was these remains which the German patrol had found on the makeshift table. A few days later the Russian counter-offensive began, and as it swept over the gallery, the group had emerged at last to engage German forces.

In the lugubrious gloom with its unspeakable odour a *Jäger* vomited. Upon finishing, he released the safety-catch of his MP-40 as he stood up, said simply, 'You filthy scum' and emptied the contents of the magazine into the two Russians. The platoon NCO ordered everybody out and they stumbled at the double through the apocalyptic tunnel to breathe the fresh, sweet air above ground.

For the veterans this was merely an episode, but it provided me with an insight into the abyss of the human state in war. It was an indication of how the Soviet political system, through its commissars, was prepared to sacrifice all vestiges of human decency in the treatment, even of its own, in the quest for victory.

There had been rumours that an order had been issued from the highest level to the effect that these political commissars were not to be afforded the status of prisoners of war if captured, and perhaps there was some obscure justification for that alleged directive being given.[3] Yet even so, that vile gallery had been a gentle, and for us, harmless initiation into what was to follow.

There was no time for deeper reflection. The important things were food and sleep, and precious little time remained before daylight came. Supported by artillery and self-propelled guns it took us another four days to wear down the Russian resistance. We retook the high ground at Voroshilovsk, but it cost us the lives of 650 German soldiers to do so. By the end of these five days I had lost what remained of my youthful innocence. The experience of the fighting to regain Voroshilovsk left its mark on my now pinched features. To judge by my reflection in the mirror I had aged ten years. At the outset my platoon had consisted of twenty men, of whom the NCO and myself were the only survivors. I had lost the feeling for time, anxiety, fear, compassion. I was a living football of events, propelled by the boot of an archaic survival instinct fuelled by the interchange of fighting, hunger, thirst and exhaustion.

On 22 July 1943 we re-established the German front line. The Russians fought with a courage born of desperation. Well camouflaged, they often displayed tremendous discipline in the field, refusing combat until within 50 metres at which distance the survivors inflicted significant casualties in our ranks, and their snipers in particular wrought havoc among the *Jäger*.

For myself I was uncomfortably aware that the sMG-gunner at the front was on a suicide mission. The tactical importance of MGs meant that they were pinpointed as priority targets in battle and received the attentions of heavy infantry weapons such as mortars and infantry guns, not to mention snipers. The losses in machine-gunners were therefore disproportionately high. The first few days at the front had made it obvious to me that my chances of surviving to my nineteenth birthday were rather slim, and depended largely upon whether I could exchange my work as a machine-gunner for another line of business at the earliest opportunity.

That same day I received a splinter wound to the left hand. One accepts such things with cool fatalism as an occupational hazard of war. To my surprise it gave me no pain and hardly bled. After testing the flexibility of my hand a few times I withdrew behind my MG to apply a field dressing. My No. 2 helped me to quickly wind the thick gauze over the gaping wound. As soon as we had finished, he yelled a warning: 'Sepp, ahead, they're coming! Shoot! Shoot!'

The pain did not set in until several hours later, by which time my platoon had been pulled out of the line and could enjoy a little peace. The field hospital assembly point was near the field kitchen. A surgeon accompanied by several assistants waited to make a preliminary inspection of reported wounds. I was directed towards a small thatched farm cottage set a short distance from the regimental HQ. Entering the field dressing station – a large marquee – I registered without emotion the groaning, whimpering, a few cries of pain and the smell of raw flesh. One of the medical corps NCOs sorted the arriving wounded according to the severity of the wound. A very young soldier was carried in on a stretcher, his now paraplegic body wobbling below a boyish face from which issued repeatedly the words, 'I can't move anything, Oh God, I can't move anything.' The medic sergeant raised the upper body, which was uninjured to the front. Between the shoulder blades gaped a wound of two hands' width through which some splintered backbone and rib segments were visible. Carefully laying the patient to rest he said: 'He is beyond help, *Junge*, with these injuries death will come as a blessing. Take him to the clergyman in the barn over there.' The barn was where the hopeless cases were brought to receive, from a visibly overcome *Wehrmacht* Catholic priest, the last rites and spiritual help in their final moments.

My own injury was classified as minor and I had to queue to be attended to. There was little privacy. A sergeant was seated nearby, his right arm bound in a handkerchief-and-stick tourniquet. The hand was attached to the forearm by a few tendons. He was clearly in shock. Whether this was considered a minor injury I had no means of knowing. My turn arrived after three hours. The duty of the medic sergeant was to cleanse and stitch flesh wounds. Without speaking he removed my dressing, examined the wound for possible foreign bodies and cleansed it with a sulphonamide solution. A very muscular medic private then seized the arm in a judo hold and turned me to obstruct my view of the wound. Immediately, and without any anaesthetic, deftly and with great skill, the sergeant began cutting the wound-edges clean before stitching. Still holding my arm in an iron grip the private advised me: 'Cry out quietly, it will help.' All my tensions and self-control now fell away and I became fully aware of the pain. As I cried I gave vent to my fury at all the inhuman experiences I had endured over the last five days.

9

The wound required fourteen days' convalescence. I was sent to regimental reserve where I could perform light duties during the healing process. G.J.R. 144 had suffered heavy casualties and was in the rear at Voroshilovsk for replenishment in personnel and material. As an apprenticed carpenter I was assigned to the regimental arsenal and given the job of sorting through a mountain of captured Russian weapons. In the second week of my convalescence I worked at repairing the stocks of damaged German carbines.

In the relative quiet and safety of the rear area I determined to accept the first chance that offered itself to avoid being returned to the front as an MG-gunner. Who knows what quirk of fate operated that I should discover in that great heap of Russian weapons a sniper's rifle which had been captured by my company and, overlooked, had not been sent on to the rear collection centre. It was a Moisin Nagant 91/30 model. At once I petitioned the chief armourer for permission to practice with the weapon. There was Russian ammunition available in plenty and the far-sighted warrant officer said: 'Show what you can do, perhaps you're a born sharpshooter. We can use men like that to keep Ivan on his toes. You know yourself how their snipers make our lives a misery.'

I grasped the opportunity gratefully and that same evening began to practice. After a few days I found that my aim was unerring. Apparently without effort I could hit a matchbox at 100 metres and the wooden lid of an ammunition box with sides 30cm long at 300 metres. The chief armourer confessed himself impressed. My wound was healing well and all too soon my fourteen days' convalescence came to an end. With orders to return to my company, I reported to the chief armourer to take my leave of him. Handing me a PU 4x magnification telescopic sight of Russian manufacture he said, 'Sepp, I have spoken to your company commander and told him about your shooting ability. He has no objection to your testing your luck as a sniper. So, *Junge*, show Ivan what you can do!'

In the first days of August 1943 I rejoined my company, my Russian sniper's rifle under my arm. When I reported to the company commander he presented me with the Wound Badge in Black and a citation saying:

Allerberger, don't think it's all behind you now. That was just a foretaste. Whatever else you do, remember to keep your arse down, particularly as a sniper. Now fall out and get Ivan annoyed.

The front was relatively quiet, activity being limited to the occasional minor artillery duel and skirmishes with reconnaissance patrols, although the pressure from Russian snipers was enormous. It was very dangerous to expose oneself momentarily, and despite the greatest precautions they regularly found a new victim. My company commander was a very open personality convinced of the advantage of having his own team of snipers and who complained bitterly at the lack of them. His was not a generally held opinion. Many officers considered the sniper to be no better than a blackguard and his craft a dishonourable and perfidious form of warfare and thus refused to have any. An officer of 3.G.D. set out his objections in his memoirs thus:

> Was he perhaps one of those marksmen who at daybreak or dusk slunk out and lay still, his gaze, like that of a cat observing a mousehole, waiting for a shoulder, a head to appear – just for a second – but long enough. A shot cracked the stillness. From a hand slowly losing its grasp there fell an empty fruit tin. The basic need which cost a man his life. Is that warfare?

In the Second World War a major problem for soldiers on active duty living rough in a confined space such as trenches was the disposal of solid excrement. It was frequently not possible to dig some form of latrine trench, and so the practice of infantrymen was to have a personal 'camping-loo', usually a large tin, which would then be emptied over the trench parapet. This action tended to expose some part of the body, and an enemy sniper would have no hesitation in accepting the opportunity to fire a bullet into it.

The lines written by the 3.G.D. officer do not reflect reality. When night fell over the respective trenches it did not bring with it a truce. Patrols tended to wander abroad at night into No-Man's-Land. The capture or killing of an enemy sentry, or the lobbing of a few grenades into the opposing trenches during such a mission had never been considered unethical in the earlier Great War. War is neither ethical nor heroic. Its purpose is to obtain a political objective by the use of maximum force in the field, and it is ultimately irrelevant to any victim whether he fell to a sniper's bullet or was ripped apart by a hand-grenade.

Once satisfied that the sniper was not outlawed by international convention, it was the 3.G.D. officers' duty to ensure that proper precautions were in place to protect their own, and then respond in kind. This raised certain ethical questions which I will tackle later. Whereas the use of the tactics described may well have been considered 'perfidious', any objection to freelance marksmen skilled in fieldcraft using their abilities to the advantage of their own side at the front seems ridiculous.

I had managed to shed my suicide job as an sMG-gunner. I was now directly responsible to the company commander, and as the situation at the time was one of defending the trenches, I was given free rein to fire at whatever target I thought fit. By instinct I did the right thing and on the first day went from trench to trench interviewing colleagues on their impressions of enemy activity, and in particular about anything observed in the adjacent 300 metres of No-Man's-Land. Everywhere I was met with a sigh of relief. 'At long last a sniper! Show them, Sepp!' An MG platoon commander took me by the sleeve and led me to a sap. For protection, the forward edge of each trench had a parapet of logs. Through a small chink between two sturdy logs he indicated the lie of the Russian trenches and told me:

In No-Man's-Land ahead of their lines there is a sniper. He has been there several days. He shoots at absolutely everything. Look, he even holed the cooking pot we raised above the parapet. Think you can get him off our backs?

Notes:

1. *Heeres-Adjutant bei Hitler 1938–1943 – Aufzeichnungen des Majors Engel*, from the Quarterly Journal of the *Institut für Zeitgeschichte* (IfZ), No. 29, Deutsche Verlags-Anstalt, Stuttgart.
2. *Jäger* = rifleman private, the basic rank of the German mountain troops in the Second World War. Also a collective term for mountain troops generally.
3. The Kommissar-Directive transformed Hitler's ideology into a practical programme, setting forth in concrete terms how the war against the Soviet Union was to be waged. In a speech to his generals on 30 March 1941 he urged that: 'With regard to the struggle against Bolshevism, we must, from the standpoint of soldierly camaraderie, turn our backs on it.' His *Guidelines for the Treatment of Political Commissars* was issued on 14 May 1941 in connection with courts-martial in the 'Barbarossa' sphere. The final version of the Directive dated 6 June 1941 was distributed to Army commanders-in-chief and Air Fleet chiefs only, with instructions that the contents were only to be passed down to the various command levels 'by word of mouth'. It ruled that 'Political commissars fighting with Soviet forces are not recognized as soldiers' and were not entitled

12

to benefit from the protective legislation applicable to prisoners of war: 'and after segregation they are to be eliminated'. See Hans-Adolf Jacobsen, '*Kommissarbefehl und Massenexecutionen sowjetischer Kriegsgefangener*', in Broszat, Jacobsen and Krausnick, *Anatomie des SS-Staates*, Vol. II, ISBN 3-423-02916-1.

Chapter 2

A Sniper
Emerges

Using the 8x magnification telescope with which the company commander had issued me, I surveyed the terrain extending from our trenches through the small gap between the parapet logs, but could make out nothing suspicious. Cautiously I raised a rolled-up field tent, topped by a peaked field cap, above the logs while I observed the Russian positions. Their sniper was probably inexperienced in the art, for he fired as soon as the field cap appeared. I saw the flash of fire from his carbine and the merest trace of smoke, and also detected the slight shimmer on the lens of his telescopic sight. Now I knew his position. In this first engagement I had already shown my intuitive feel for the sniper's role. I made a mental note of the first rule of sniper combat: never fire at anything not positively identified. When allowed to fire at will, loose off only one shot from a lair, then either change location or at least desist temporarily from further activity and conceal yourself.

My opponent remained where he was, awaiting a fresh opportunity – a fatal error for which he was to pay with his life. I placed the rolled tent on the parapet ledge as a rest for the forestock and cautiously poked the muzzle of my carbine through the observation gap between the logs. I could not use the telescopic sight because the crack was too narrow. The Russian was about 90 metres away, within effective range for the weapon's fixed sights.

I felt very nervous. The *Jäger* were expecting a super-precise shot, and I was now confronted with the task, for the first time in my life, of deliberately aiming to kill a man 'in cold blood'. Was this scrupulous? My throat was dry, my heart raced and while aiming the weapon I noticed how it trembled in my hands. I could not fire the shot in this condition and held back, taking several deep breaths to compose myself. Colleagues surrounded me, watching with expectation. What could be worse? I settled the weapon into my shoulder once more, aimed carefully and hesitated. 'What are you waiting for? Let him have it,' somebody said from several yards away. This evaporated my tension. In a dream and with machine-like precision I began to curl my trigger finger. Taking up the pressure I breathed in, held my breath and squeezed. The rifle cracked, a thick wisp of smoke drifted across the field of fire, obscuring my vision. A *Jäger* watching through another slit in the parapet logs shouted, 'You got him, man, right between the eyes. He's dead.' The news of the death of the Russian sniper spread like a forest fire through the trenches. Suddenly MGs began to bark, carbines cracked and somebody yelled, 'Attack!' The Russians, completely surprised by our activity and the sudden assault by German troops, fled their advanced trenches for their main front line. We reached the abandoned positions without encountering resistance.

In curiosity, a group of us made a short detour for the hide from where the Russian sniper had been operating, a scattered pile of logs beneath which he had dug a hollow – now a shallow open grave – for his body. Beside his feet was a trail of blood. Two *Jäger* dragged the body free by the ankles. The Russian was a boy of about sixteen with crew-cut hair. The bullet had entered through his right eye. A bloody mash of brain and bone splinters covered his upper torso at the back, the fist-sized exit wound in his head revealed that his skull had been cleaned of cerebral matter by the pressure wave of the rifle bullet. 'You hit him cleanly with a single shot, dear boy, and over open sights at almost a hundred metres. You're good, Sepp,' a *Jäger* commented. I stared at my victim with a mixture of pride, revulsion and bad conscience. All at once my stomach revolted and I vomited up my most recent meal of black bread, sardines in oil, and malt coffee. My colleagues reacted with sympathy and understanding for my lack of control. A blue-eyed NCO, ten years my senior in years, head and shoulders above me in height and wearing a large reddish beard, comforted me with a striking north German accent: 'No need to be ashamed, old man, it has happened to the best of us. You just have to get over it. Better to sick up than shit your pants. As it happens, Papa has a remedy ...' and at that he withdrew a silvery schnapps flask from a breast pocket and offered me a slug. I took a mouthful and handed it back, thinking as I did so, 'He looks like a Viking, the only things missing are the horns on his helmet.' The idea of a Viking serving with the mountain troops amused me and made me smile.

By now the Soviets had gathered their wits and had begun a counter-attack. An hour later we were all back in the positions we had occupied earlier. I had passed the sniper's practical and was now accepted in the role by all and sundry. The admiration this engendered enabled me to shrug off the feelings of revulsion I still felt for my deed. I made a mental note of the second rule of sniper-fieldcraft:

War is a merciless system of Killing and Being Killed. In action, sympathy for the enemy is ultimately suicide, for every opponent whom you do not kill can turn the tables and kill you. Your chances of survival are measured by the yardstick of how you compare in skill and objectivity as against your opponent.

This was a principle to which I remained true throughout. If I had an enemy in the crosswires of my telescopic sight and a finger on the trigger, his fate was sealed.

That same day I killed two other careless Russians. In youthful pride at my success I used my pocket-knife to make three notches in the stock of my rifle, a ritual I kept up while I had my Russian sniper-rifle, and not until the death of a fellow sniper in action a year later did I abandon this suicidal habit. The same day, the *Spiess* (Company Sergeant Major or CSM) told me that every kill claimed required a witness in the shape of an officer or NCO with the company command. Those kills outside offensive and defensive manoeuvres in the fighting for trench positions would not count. I had to keep a small pocket book listing my kills and these also had to be confirmed by an officer or NCO. For every ten confirmed kills I would receive a 7cm long and 1cm wide strip of silver trim, such as NCOs wore along the edge of the jacket collar, and these were to be sewn on the lower left sleeve.[1] Yet the obtaining of confirmation was often a difficult business. Many NCOs envied a sniper his success and refused to sign. Artillery spotters, especially young officers full of military idealism, considered *Wehrmacht* snipers as loathsome assassins and used the opportunity to express their undisguised antipathy by declining their signature. This was also the reason why few artillery spotters and snipers ever cooperated. Another reason for the institutional antipathy was the practice of snipers to dress up dummies in the garb of artillery spotters to lure enemy snipers' fire: we had the unofficial acquisition of tents and items from officers' uniforms off to a fine art.

Over the ensuing fourteen days I scored another twenty-seven kills. My new career was rapidly becoming routine, although as a greenhorn I had a certain amount of luck. My Russian counterparts had classified me as competent and tended to avoid my field of fire, and so our company's sector of the front remained relatively quiet. This gave me the opportunity to learn from my mistakes in the field, an advantage denied many other newcomers lacking battle experience who had been required to pay with their lives for a minor oversight.

On or about 18 August 1943, the long days of waiting came to an abrupt end. Days previous the Soviets had stepped up their artillery bombardment culminating in a major offensive the entire length of the Donetz front. Impressively superior in numbers they had soon penetrated the main German front line. We abandoned our positions and, on the defensive, I was able to demonstrate how a good sniper could be of outstanding tactical significance. Although I had been at the front less than two months, I had the stoical calm and cold-bloodedness of the veteran infantryman. Even in very dangerous situations I found I could keep my nerve and fight as if inspired. I was endowed with the skill of the warrior, something which theory cannot pass down and which even the best training school is unable to inculcate. Battle proves the soldier in the mastery of personal fear and the natural impulse to turn and run!

On 27 August 1943 Hitler returned to his former FHQ 'Wehrwolf' in woodland north of Vinnitsa where he met *Generalfeldmarschall* von Manstein, commanding general, Army Group South. The message was not a pleasant one for Hitler's ears. If Manstein could not be guaranteed another twelve divisions immediately, he would have to evacuate the Donetz Basin. Since these did not exist, Hitler gave his tacit permission in promising him 'all units which can be made available'. He then returned to FHQ *Wolfsschanze* in East Prussia.

3.G.D. began a systematic and orderly retreat to the Dnieper about 200 kilometres to the south-west. Matching thirty-three divisions against the ten of the German side, bled of personnel and weapons, the Russians headed this vastly superior force towards the German lines where every kilometre was defended by no more than ninety infantrymen. To close the gaps, logistical and other rearward units were thrown forward. We had no reserves, nor strength in depth. If the Soviets breached the front, the effect would be immediate and calamitous. 3.G.D. was at the heart of the heaviest fighting, at Saporyshe, where two separate Soviet columns were attempting to break through on the flanks in a pincer movement. Although G.J.R. 144 was faced by an enemy ten times stronger at the strategically important locations, the line of resistance held and afforded other units the opportunity to fall back and regroup.[2] Frequently shifting strongpoints, the Russian offensive ground on for weeks until at last, in September, the unpaved main highways and roads were transformed into a knee-deep impassable morass by the early onset of the incessant rains of autumn. Chronic lack of sleep, problems of bringing up munitions and food, and the pressure to fight, fight and keep fighting made unceasing demands on our last physical reserves. It characterized our daily situation, and remained the standard for the remainder of the war.

My company, 7./144, was ordered to cover the regiment's withdrawal. Sixty *Jäger* occupied a village at a strategically important crossroads in order to hold back the Russian motorized advance. Enemy reconnaissance quickly established the pitifully small strength of the unit. The Soviets encircled us and stood poised to wipe us out. 7./144 was a veteran and well-disciplined fighting force. Well dug in and with accurate defensive fire, we kept the Russians at a distance. Even tank and anti-tank rounds presented us with few problems in our foxholes. It was in battles such as this one that the sniper's hour arrived. At ranges up to 300 metres shot after shot found its billet. At the focal point of all our battles I made my appearance and forced the enemy on the defensive by my almost infallible shooting. My nerves were of steel. I knew this for sure as each projectile found its way with deadly certainty into the Russian ranks. In these desperate encounters, it gave us a decisive edge if one could undermine the enemy's fighting spirit. The experienced sniper therefore aimed less for fatal hits than for hits to the torso, which put a man out of action and left him screaming in agony.

The scheme of a Russian attack was to send forward their troops in waves. The first two waves would usually be armed, the rear two waves often weaponless. As the first two waves were cut down, the rear attackers advanced over the corpses of their comrades, availing themselves of the weapons no longer needed by the dead. This was an interesting strategy that must have had an unenviable effect on their troops' morale. After some thought, I developed my own response to perfection. I would bide my time until the four waves were on their way towards our lines, then open rapid fire into the

18

two rear waves, aiming for the stomach. The unexpected casualties at the rear and the terrible cries of the most seriously wounded tended to collapse the rear lines and so disconcert the two leading ranks that the whole attack would begin to falter. At this point I could now concentrate on the two leading waves, dispatching those Soviets closer than 50 metres with a shot to the heart or the head. Enemy soldiers who had turned and run I transformed into men screaming with pain with a shot to the kidneys. At this, an attack would frequently disintegrate altogether. In such an engagement I would often fire off more than twenty rounds, none of which counted towards my final total of kills. In this manner over two days, in cooperation with comrades, I played my part in saving 7./144. On the second night, the company escaped the encirclement, taking with it thirteen wounded. I held the rear, keeping the pursuers at a respectful distance with accurate sniper fire until, at first light, we re-established contact with our main front line. The question of ethics and honour involved in my tactics is open to question, but against such an enemy as the Soviets, who had no hesitation in slaughtering the prisoners they took, and outnumbered us ten to one, I considered it justified in the circumstances.

Reaching the precarious safety of our battle line did not mean that we could have a good rest. At daylight the Russians attacked anew, although they seemed cautious. They had a new ruse, sending forward three T-34s supported by infantry, and from cover we listened to the monsters trundling in our direction. I had dug a hollow along our defensive line of improvised positions, which the infantry had done their best to camouflage. At about 150 metres from our trenches the leading T-34 jolted to a sudden stop. The turret rotated with an audible hum and the gun swept the terrain as if sniffing for us. When the turret stopped, the hatch opened a few seconds later. I aimed the crosswires of my telescopic sight at the lid. A head protruded two hands'-breadth above the rim, and a pair of hands raised binoculars to the head's eyes. I had calibrated my weapon on a pinpoint at 120 metres – if he raised himself much higher I would be bound to score. In this situation it was absolutely essential that the shot was good, for it would signal the fire-fight to begin. I hesitated briefly, during which time it occurred to me that this individual was probably not only the commander of the tank, but possibly of the entire attack. His death might decide the affair in our favour. I took a deep breath, concentrated, put myself into a calm

19

frame of mind, drew back the trigger evenly, and the shot cracked out. Through the sight I saw a torrent of blood spatter the hatch lid, after which the head disappeared. Seconds later everybody began firing. The three tanks, immobile, rained a harmless fire above our lines: after a few minutes their motors started up and the colossi reversed, confirming my assumption. The Soviet attack was now leaderless, and when the Soviet follow-up began an hour later it lacked impetus and conviction. A single bullet had rendered the enemy assault literally headless and in all probability enabled us to ward it off. The offensive petered out on 20 September by which time the German front had been shortened, consolidated, and the enemy break-through prevented thanks to the fighting spirit of 3.G.D. In the bitter fighting, 7./144 lost more than half its complement. The survivors were exhausted and lice-infested, the majority either wounded or sick. The superhuman struggle they had waged for insignificant, nameless areas on a map was etched into their faces. Personally I had come through unscathed, except for the lice, and diarrhoea occasioned by a recent staple diet of salted gherkins found in an outhouse on a Russian farm.

During the lull, the division erected the Wotan Line. This temporary front induced in us a nostalgia for home, being a territory once inhabited by Volga-Germans long since deported by the Soviets. The small, neat towns and villages had names like Heidelberg, Tiefenbrunn and Rosenberg: the houses had been abandoned but left in such good order, with cooking utensils hanging neatly in cupboards, that it looked for all the world like the former occupants would return at any moment. We dug in, mindful that within a few days or weeks the hurricane of destruction would sweep over it all. It was here that we experienced the first ugly premonitions of what was to befall our own nation – an omen of what lay ahead.

While the Red Army regrouped for a new offensive, G.J.R. 144 was near Gendelberg, its inadequate numbers swelling with convalescents and those returning from leave. The supply of weapons and ammunition to us was well below expectations. All the more essential had it therefore become to conduct a thorough reconnaissance of the terrain and identify the places where an enemy attack was likely to be focused, and accordingly where our own limited forces should best be located. It was of equal importance to deceive the enemy as to our meagre numbers by daring raids. Each early morning and at dusk I was to be found scouting ahead of our lines. It was my purpose to keep unwary

Russian forward patrols away from our lines by surprise accurate fire, to decimate their numbers and drive the survivors back to their own trenches in disarray. The usual patrol they sent out had the single objective of spotting our positions and in general they did not expect to run up against a lone sniper well out into No-Man's-Land. When they did, it tended to stun them momentarily, allowing me to rapidly shoot dead a number of the party before they either gathered their wits sufficiently to find cover or withdrew to a safe distance.

So it was that at dawn one beautiful autumn morning in late September I lay well disguised on the wooded summit of a small hill observing a Russian artillery emplacement no more than a kilometre distant, when from a copse about 150 metres away there came into a clearing directly along my line of sight, a Russian patrol led by a boyish lieutenant. The platoon appeared not to have a care in the world and waddled along like a gaggle of geese in the sunshine. With due presence of mind, careful not to betray my lair, I moved my rifle into position and through the scope watched the undisciplined troop below me. I determined that the officer probably came from highly placed Russian political circles, for contrary to normal practice he wore a tailor-made uniform of the finest cloth and wonderful boots of best leather. Spellbound by the scene, finger on the trigger, I saw the lieutenant suddenly stumble as he caught his foot against the exposed root of a tree. After regaining his balance and composure, he withdrew from a pocket a white handkerchief with embroidered edging and proceeded to wipe his fingers and flick at the dust on his boots. For weeks I had been in the closest association with filth, vile stenches and fleas, locked in a daily ruthless struggle for survival, and I saw the humour of the situation. Alas, there was no place for sentimentality in this war. To spare this platoon of kids might still have led indirectly to immediate danger for myself and my regiment. While the lieutenant carefully shook the handkerchief and folded it meticulously before replacing it in his breast pocket, I aimed the crosswires of the telescopic sight at his heart. With a morbid inner smile I reflected on the ritual now unfolding, the poetic art of killing known to the Japanese Samurai in their Bushido, and with a strange lightness of heart squeezed the trigger for the lieutenant's finale.

While the sound was still cracking the morning stillness, the young officer looked with horror at the hole in his chest, from which a small fountain of blood was pulsing. While his platoon ran shouting in panic in all directions, he sank slowly to his knees, his eyes looked for the last time to the sky and then he toppled sideways into the undergrowth. After I shot dead two of his men imprudently attempting to drag him back into the clearing, the others elected to remain in concealment and eventually withdrew without ever knowing from whence the fatal shots came. I knew of course that my lair had outlived its purpose and, like the phantom of the woods, quickly made myself scarce.

My scouting activity had given me a good idea of how the enemy was massing his forces. My reports, and those made by other snipers, were an important part of the mosaic of German short-range reconnaissance, predicting the focal points of the impending offensive.

At eight on the morning of 26 September 1943, hundreds of lightning flashes lit the eastern horizon with a diabolical light. A growling howl neared the German positions and swelled to a deafening roar as the abyss of hell opened. The cargo of hundreds of guns and Stalin organs merged into a single developing explosion: the air sighed with splinters and flying chunks of earth. Gas and dust made it difficult to breathe. As the first wave of explosions died away, a maximum of self-control was required as we heard the shattering screams of the wounded and mutilated. We cowered into our trenches and foxholes as deeply as we could: some offered prayers or silent petitions for mercy, others grabbed at hysterical comrades bent on making a run for it in the open. Under the impact of high explosives the earth trembled. The air developed into a suffocating mix of dirt, gases and metal splinters. Helpless as a child I assumed the foetal position in my foxhole. A gigantic explosion nearby deafened and confused me momentarily. I looked up to see a great shower of earth and a dark object flying towards me over the trench parapet. Instinctively as I ducked my head the object thudded down in the filth. I recoiled in horror. The steaming remains of a comrade from the adjacent trench, a torso without limbs, its chest, neck and face ripped by metal splinters into a bloody, amorphous mass, had come to join me. The mouth of the thing, surprisingly unhurt, began to groan and a gutteral voice spoke as if from another world: 'What happened? Why is it so dark? Why can't I feel my body any more?' Unable to understand, the stumps of the upper arms shrugged helplessly. 'Help me,' the remains implored with a gurgle. Panic seized me. Almost in hysteria I kept to the trench wall so as not to have to touch the mutilated torso. The moribund object began to cry, but in answer to my prayers he soon died. Deaf to the hellish backdrop of tank guns and mortars I attempted to compose myself, for the infantry attack was imminent.

As abruptly as it had begun a half hour before, the barrage stopped, to be replaced by the rattle of tank tracks and the 'Hurrah!' of the approaching Russian infantry. In a split-second we emerged from our shock. While medics attended the seriously wounded, those of us still in a condition to fight raised our rifles to the trench parapets and returned the Russian fire. With deadly accuracy, round after round from my carbine found a billet in the ranks of the attackers. The barrel grew so hot that the anti-rust grease melted and dripped over my fingers. Shells continued to pound our lines and the air was thick with metal splinters. I was mobile, moving from trench to trench, always seeking cover, snatching ammunition from dead Russians who had almost made it. Along a small sector of the front there seemed little sense to it all; our objective was mere survival. The individual soldier knew nothing of the greater scheme in which this Russian offensive was linked to their attempt to break through our lines at the lower Dnieper. For eight long days the battle raged, constantly switching between attack, defence and counter-attack. German companies and regiments melted away, lacking reserves. The dressing stations worked day and night. An unending chain of buckets full of human tissue and amputated limbs made the trip to waste trenches behind the operating tents. Hundreds of men waited for their turn under the knife, groaning, crying, dying. The medics were quite ruthless in segregating out the hopeless cases: some met death in a state of morphine intoxication, but the majority died alone and in agony. Many of the most hopeless cases were put out of their misery where they lay if the danger existed that they might fall into Soviet hands, for the enemy practised diabolical tortures of the wounded as a matter of routine.

It was in this environment, as a youth of nineteen years, that I lost what remained of my innocence. I determined to sell my life as dearly as possible and in doing so developed an extraordinary professionalism. I kept my nerve where others succumbed to panic. I used my sniper's rifle as a surgical weapon – with deadly precision. I had the feel for battle, knew the rhythm of defence, cover, attack. My lack of fear for injury and death amounted to a state of mind that one calls bravery. It is one of the strange things about war that a few soldiers appear invulnerable to serious injury or death. I was one of these, and there can be no doubt that Hitler also had this same gift of avoiding serious injury at the front, living a charmed life in the trenches of the Western Front from 1914 to 1918.

On 4 October 1943 the fighting abated, allowing our exhausted and much reduced force a few days to regroup. Five days later the Red Army resumed its attack on what remained of 3.G.D., which it outnumbered by twenty to one. The obligatory artillery barrage began at ten in the morning. Four hundred batteries and 220 Stalin organs pounded our lines with 15,000 exploding projectiles per hour. The division went to ground, and when it stopped, men came forth like zombies out of the steaming sulphuric air and churned earth surrounding their positions. In despair they readied themselves, each *Jäger* a true soldier hewn from the granite rock of self-control, battle experience, dourness and determination to come through. Like a flood wave the Russian soldiers of foot came towards them. Their reserve of expendable men seemed inexhaustible. While the *Wehrmacht* units, composed of all there was and no reserves, shrank ever smaller, the Red Army grew ever larger. In this it was helped, in no small measure, by the Japanese decision not to pressurize the Siberian frontier and so allow its defenders to be transferred to the Russian western front. Moreover, every male aged between fourteen and sixty was conscripted without exemption.

Many of the units were intended as simple cannon fodder, being stuffed into an Army greatcoat over their civilian clothes and given two days' weapons training. So hasty was this process that there were insufficient arms to go round, and there came into being the tactics whereby the leading attack wave would be armed with rifles or machine pistols while the rear waves left the trenches unarmed, being required to pick up the weapon of a fallen front-wave soldier on the traverse towards the German lines. The danger in this proceeding must have been obvious even to the simple-minded, and the Russian Army Command solved it by having NKVD secret service troops (the secret police) on hand to forcibly clear the trenches at the word of command. During this attack I witnessed at first hand how the Russian waverers and doubters were simply shot down from behind while the others headed for the German lines as if confronting nothing more worrisome than a heavy shower of hail. For us it was a rabbit shoot, the terrain before us a killing field of indescribable size with walls of Russian dead and seriously wounded. The corpses piled up, often towering higher than the height of a man. The rear-wave attackers had to climb up the dead who were incidentally useful as bullet-traps since they provided cover, and prevented us continuing to fire into the rear ranks. Sometimes the dead were stacked so high that the attack would begin to peter out and tanks had to be brought up to plough a way through, no consideration being given to the screams of the wounded during this activity. The tracks of the T-34s squashed down the cadavers, cracking bones like dry twigs. It was like watching bulldozers flattening a rubbish tip composed of a humanity, some of which was still living, and screamed and cursed in its death agony. The battle escalated: when some of the attackers finally got through after we ran short of ammunition, they were repulsed with bayonet and sharpened entrenching tool. Our defence was berserk enough to ensure that by evening the Russian attack, lacking numbers, disintegrated.

Notes:

1. If this tradition had been maintained, leading sniper Hetzenauer would have had thirty-four, and Allerberger twenty-five such strips on the lower left arm of the uniform jacket by war's end.
2. 3.G.D. was mainly Austrian and not German. 5.SS-Div. 'Wiking', composed mainly of non-German volunteers, made the bitter complaint about having this same 'fire-fighter' role foisted upon it, giving permanent cover and so allowing other racially German forces the opportunity to escape.

Chapter 3

A Taste of Trench Warfare at Nikopol

I was under the immediate instructions of my company commander and found myself repeatedly at the centre of the fighting. The distance between ourselves and the enemy often shortened so swiftly that I put aside my sniper's rifle after a few rounds in favour of the MP-40. I always carried the machine pistol slung across my back for those difficult situations in which the front lines dissolved into a general mêlée. Under 30 metres the telescopic sight was only of limited use because the visual field it offered was too narrow. Aiming over open sights below the telescopic mounting was also impractical because the sight masked most of the field. These situations were very awkward for the sniper. He had to keep a close hold on two weapons and because of it ran a special danger of being identified as a sniper, and accordingly a priority target.

Fighting would die down towards evening but the tension rarely fell away, for the Russians made no secret of their moves to reorganize and we knew that a resumption of activity was only a few hours away. Here the sniper was particularly valuable, for with the occasional well-aimed, long-range shot he could force the enemy to maintain his distance.

During the night of 10 October 1943 the Russians broke off their fire on our sector, and in a few minutes a suspicious lull occurred. The company commander used the situation to make a swift inspection of the trenches and gather reports. *Jäger* in a forward trench reported unusual movements in the bushy terrain before them, and an eight-man veteran patrol was assembled. I accompanied them as escort, creeping through the wasteland with great caution about 30 metres away on their flank. I carried my sniper's rifle, the patrol carried MPs and hand-grenades. Their movement forward was through knee-high grass towards a spot which had been indicated as suspect. After about 300 metres we heard the sound of muffled voices. At a signal from the platoon leader I found myself a well-hidden lair amongst a clump of bushes, raised my rifle and surveyed the area through the sight. About 80 metres ahead I could vaguely make out a depression like a small valley. The patrol worked forward on the edges of this depression, and when the patrol leader investigated below he espied a battle group of about a hundred Russian soldiers, old men and boys, probably under the leadership of an inexperienced political commissar. Anxious and uncertain, they were huddled together chattering and smoking. The platoon sergeant crept back and used hand signs to explain his discovery. One slipped over to my position, informing me that despite being heavily outnumbered, at first light the platoon would make an attack. It was hoped that this would drive the surprised Russians instinctively towards the exit from the depression where I would be waiting to pick them off.

To the east the sky lightened slightly two hours later. Many of the Russians had fallen asleep, those on watch visibly not vigilant. At a signal from the platoon leader each *Jäger* took up three stick grenades and primed them. As if from nowhere, the twenty four grenades exploded virtually simultaneously among the Red soldiers, who at once broke out in panic. Those who had not been seriously wounded ran blindly in all directions, firing into the darkness, which resulted in further casualties to their own side. The screams of the wounded rent the air. Calmly the *Jäger* aimed and fired their machine-pistols into the leaderless rabble. As expected, the Russians slowed towards the exit to the depression, and straight into the crosswires of my carbine. It was a routine massacre: aim at the chest, quickly but smoothly pull the trigger, repeat, aim, fire. Round after round found its goal with deadly certainty. Five were already dead, sprawled across the grass. When the others hesitated it gave me time to reload another clip. Before they could recover, the next five joined their comrades. The remainder turned back to be met by the MP-fire and grenades of the patrol. It moved back and forth like this between the depression exit and the sink for several minutes before the butchery reached its conclusion. We had sustained no casualties or wounded. We left behind us a heap of mutilated bodies, and the cries of the wounded and dying. Patrol and sniper vanished without a sound like spirits of the mist in the grey light of early morning.

This brave surprise raid, not without its share of luck, afforded our decimated company a few extra hours of deceptive peace. But at midday the Russian counter-blow hit us with undiminished force. With courage born of despair we held out until evening. The Russians called it off at dusk, and shortly before midnight we learnt that the Russians had finally broken through along another sector of the front and were assembling their forces to concentrate on widening and deepening the breach there. For our company it meant salvation. We had become so weak that we would not have been able to withstand a single extra day of it. Hunger, exhaustion, wounds and infections had all taken their toll, and we needed rest desperately. For days we had feasted on nothing but salted gherkins and apples discovered in Russian farm outhouses, and the toughest intestines were no match for this lethal mixture. Everybody had diarrhoea.

We were given a week to take a breather, sleep, clean ourselves and our apparel. Hygiene is an aspect of military good order that cannot be underestimated. During basic training and while in barracks, the *Wehrmacht* had regular and unannounced hygiene inspections, which included the genital region. These were carried out by a staff surgeon and several medic NCOs. In the dining hall we paraded and stripped naked. The doctors were especially keen on detecting the earliest indications of sexual diseases, inflammations and conditions caused by uncleanliness. To have unclean genitals was a disciplinary offence, and if an impending inspection was suspected, no effort was spared to bring the region involved up to scratch. In action, every opportunity had to be taken to maintain bodily hygiene, the alternative being a number of unpleasant medical conditions and tiny unwelcome visitors.

On 21 October 1943 the Russians launched a fresh assault. Despite a number of successful holding actions and counter-attacks, they gained territory. Throwing the main German battle line into chaotic disorder, contact was lost between units, and a highly unstable situation developed. For me, the picture was totally confused. In my dugout, in a mixture of fascination and fear, I watched two Red soldiers enter a neighbouring trench, whose occupants had run out of ammunition. The first Russian fell when an entrenching tool split his head open, but the other proved himself a fantastic bayonet fighter. With catlike agility he parried every effort of the six *Jäger* to put him down. In the wild mêlée I was never able to obtain a clear enough view of the Russian soldier to shoot him, and I witnessed how one after another he disposed of his opponents. He was a veteran whose single-minded determination brought him success, and their combined efforts were insufficient to overwhelm him. They seemed to lack conviction and offered individual, and not coordinated, resistance to the intruder. It seemed almost as if they went to their doom spellbound. The last survivor put up the best struggle, and this gave me the opportunity to shoot. As the Russian lunged with the final deadly thrust, his face passed momentarily into the crosswires and I fired. The German infantryman stared almost incomprehendingly at the burst head of the Russian, destroyed by an explosive round. Bone fragments and strips of cerebellum had sprayed the German's face and uniform. A combination of fear and relief at his unexpected salvation seized the man. Inspired by a new will to live, he sprinted for my dugout, and made it.

This incident exemplifies what is required of the good sniper. More than practical shooting ability he needs a high degree of self-discipline enabling him to respond correctly to apparently hopeless situations. In action the military sniper is more valuable for precise and sure weapons handling in routine infantry combat than laying in wait for a single kill. For this reason, by tradition snipers had always been recruited from among veterans in the field rather than from green marksmen steeped in theory. The career of a young sniper fresh from training was fifteen to twenty rounds on average before he fell in action. The principal reasons for failure were: choice of hide lacking secure escape route beyond view of enemy; aversion to zigzag sprints through enemy mortar fire; firing too many rounds from the same position. If a sniper was spotted, as a rule he came under fire from enemy heavy infantry weapons. Under mortar fire without the opportunity to withdraw unseen, his only option was to sprint. This was dubbed *Hasensprung* – 'the hare's jump' – and involved suddenly leaping up to dart in wild irregular zigzags to the nearest dugout. The run through enemy fire required great presence of mind and nerves of steel. Inexperienced snipers who remained quaking in their boots were soon killed off.

Despite the great efforts of 3.G.D., the Red Army made such inroads to the south of the division that an encirclement threatened. 6.Army was split in two, enforcing an immediate retreat to the far banks of the Dnieper to establish a new defensive line and ward off disaster. As usual, *Oberkommando des Heeres* or OKH (German Army High Command) deliberated far too long, and when the order to fall back on the Dnieper finally came on 31 October 1943, the Russians had already driven a broad wedge through the German front and were poised for the decisive thrust. At Nikopol a bridgehead was to be set up to keep open the manganese mines and ensure the production and supply of the ore for as long as possible. The bridgehead was composed of nine divisions including 3.G.D., all reduced to about a quarter of their authorized size in men and materials. We were allowed three weeks to dig in and organize our defences. Supplies were resumed, but only in modest quantities, and included a supplementary item of uniform in the shape of cotton-padded reversible camouflage suits, one side white for snow conditions, the other having a camouflage pattern. Our initial joy at this issue of warm winter apparel quickly evaporated. The thin outer material tore easily. It was not impermeable, and during rainfall the padding became saturated, making the suit uncomfortably heavy and destroying its protective effect against low temperatures. In really low temperatures, the cotton froze. The new fur-lined boots had similar drawbacks and additionally provided parasites with an idyllic environment.

The suits were useful only when the wearer was required to remain immobile in dry cold. The voluminous cut enabled it to be worn over the field-grey uniform, but here one sweated profusely at the least exertion, and since the material was impermeable it gave rise to colds and associated disorders. Once the warmer weather set in, hundreds of discarded suits finished their useful life strewn along the route of the division's retreat. Thus the theme of cotton-type camouflage suits was resolved for the duration by 3.G.D. We were much better served by warm underwear, blankets and tents. In the spring of 1944 I persuaded the regimental tailor to make me a camouflage smock from a tent, and this served me well for a long period. I also had a light, white camouflage suit made for the snow. This was easy to roll up and carry. The thin cotton was so light that it did not interfere with my movements even when wet, and it dried as quickly as the smock.

The enemy's activity at this juncture was limited to surprise raids and sniper fire. I went out hunting daily, the occasional deadly round disquieting the Russian lines. For this purpose I used the burnt-out ruin of a T-34 in No-Man's-Land as a safe hide. At daybreak I slid below the vehicle body, which afforded me excellent protection. I could observe and fire on the Russian trenches through a hole in the tracks. Contrary to practice, I used this position for four days and fired five rounds. The Russians had no heavy weapons and I felt absolutely safe beneath the wreck of the steel colossus. The enemy became extremely cautious and since it was becoming more difficult for me to find a target, on the fifth day I took an observer with me. The choice fell on Balduin Moser, a Tyrolean, whom I had befriended several weeks before. As we set out before dawn that morning for my armoured hide-out, we had no foreboding of what lay in store for us. My error had been to fire from that secure position too often, and the Russians had identified it as my location on the grounds that there was nothing else remotely likely in the neighbourhood. Up to this point the Soviets had not stationed any artillery in this sector, and had been defenceless against me. However, in response to their discovery they had called on a sniper of their own to nail me. He was now lying in wait for his opportunity.

The morning sun glinted as it rose above the eastern horizon and threw its first rays across the barren steppe. Balduin and I had settled in below the T-34 and were now carefully scrutinizing the enemy positions for a victim, perhaps one recently arisen from his sack and emptying his fruit tin over the trench parapet without a thought for the possible dangers. Probably it was no more than the merest reflected glint of sunlight from binoculars projected a little too far forward which alerted the Russian sniper to the fact that our position was occupied. Aiming the crosswires of his telescopic sight at the spot where he had seen the flash of sunlight, in his well-camouflaged position he awaited his opportunity. Seconds later he fired. It so happened that we identified each other in the same instant, for Balduin was whispering to me: 'Two fingers right near the little hump there's a movem... .'

The bullet struck the binoculars in Balduin's hands and exploded against his mouth, destroying the lower part of his face. He stared at me in panic, gurgling blood. A second round exploded between us on the ground. I dived for the darkest corner and pulled Balduin towards me by the ankles. We were stuck here until nightfall, any attempt to leave our hiding place would mean certain death at the hands of this sniper. As for my wounded friend I was completely helpless. This was not a case for a first aid dressing or tourniquet but the soonest possible professional help from a surgeon. The remains of Balduin's tongue had swollen to the size of a child's ball and was blocking the airway. My attempt to force the tongue to one side caused him to

31

retch and made breathing more difficult. Only a tube or a tracheotomy could save him now. I resigned myself to watching him die. Breathing gradually became more difficult to him and eventually he drowned in his own blood. At the end he gave me one last, sad look, offered me a final handshake, and then died in my arms. I maintained a death watch over Balduin until night fell. When it was quite dark, I pulled the body out from below the tank and carried my friend back to the trenches, made a brief report to the company commander and handed him Balduin's identity tags. Next morning we dug the grave. In the treeless steppe there was no wood for a cross, and so after the interment his steel helmet was laid on the mound. The same night the wreck of the T-34 was wired for explosives, and blown up next morning, the purpose being to avoid having the Russians shell it and so endanger our trenches. A few days later the next Russian offensive swept forward and obliterated the last resting place of Balduin Moser.

On 20 November 1943 the Russians attacked on a modest scale, which presented no problem for the defenders. Nevertheless they had to be watched closely, and casualties weakened our fighting strength. On the night of 25 November they concentrated especially on the sector defended by 3.G.D., throwing forward 200 tanks and several regiments of infantry. G.J.R. 144 was faced by fifty tanks.

We were roused from sleep at five that morning by an artillery barrage of one hour's duration. We had no anti-tank weapons to hold off two armoured brigades and infantry riding on the tank hulls. The tanks rolled across the G.J.R. 144 lines, and once behind us the infantry disembarked, quickly knocking out battalion and company headquarters and rear supply areas. The second wave consisted of flame-thrower tanks. The smell of burning and scorched flesh and the infernal screaming of the suffering was a terrible demoralizing factor. Our command structure broke down and each unit fought for itself down to the last bayonet and knife. For hundreds of *Jäger*, death came in the cruellest circumstances. No prisoners were taken and the wounded were treated with the utter barbarity one had come to expect of the Russians.

One could accept the artillery barrage as a kind of natural cataclysm to which one was exposed and helpless. But the steady creaking, mechanical approach of the deadly tank force, accompanied by the blast of countless enemy mortars, chilled the heart of the bravest, and the impulse to turn and run was difficult to resist. As the tanks approached, through binoculars I had carefully scrutinized the infantry riding the hulls in an effort to identify the commander, either by his clothing or weapons. Only when the Russians were within 100 metres did we receive the order to fire. At once I fired at as many tanks as possible. Veteran Soviet soldiers would recognize the danger at once, jump down and seek cover behind the vehicle: this had the effect of slowing down the attack. Those who remained sitting where they were got a fatal bullet for their trouble. The last act was always to fire into the reserve fuel tank at the rear of the T-34. With any luck, the fuel would spill through the ventilation slots into the engine where it would frequently ignite. This fire would stop the tank in its tracks, so to speak. We were shooting for our very lives, but no matter how enormous their casualties, this Russian wave was going to break through, for we had too few anti-tank guns and light mortars. The distance soon reduced to the point where we could see their faces. Confronted by a withering fire from our trenches, the Russian foot soldiers held back a wary 100 metres while twenty T-34s rolled ever closer with a menacing growl. We prepared the few hollow charges we had. Our other anti-tank weapon was stick grenades in tied bundles. Placed in a tank's wheels, they would often blow the track apart, thus rendering the vehicle unmanoeuvrable. Unfortunately these defensive measures required the infantryman to be in the closest of contact with the T-34, a procedure that called for a high degree of commitment and bravery. When a tank got to within 10 metres of our lines its field of fire was masked and presented the defenders with the opportunity to approach. They had to be nimble, for if the tank crew spotted the trench, they would manoeuvre across it, twisting and turning the tank so as to collapse it and bury the occupants alive. For this reason, only battle-hardened veterans were trusted with anti-tank devices.

As the Russian tanks passed the critical distance, our selected *Jäger* snaked towards them on their bellies, sprang up and attempted to place the charge against the turret, engines or in the wheels. Only a few made it that far, however, for the Russian infantry spared no effort to thwart them in the endeavour. Five of the colossi fell victim to explosions sufficient to immobilize them, but the other fifteen rattled and screeched through our lines as we cowered low in our foxholes and trenches. Not every man kept his nerve. Now and again someone would take to his heels in an attempt to flee the danger, only to be mown down by the Russian infantry. I watched as a comrade

30 metres away made a run in wild zigzags towards a neighbouring trench. Fifteen metres short his legs were riddled by an MG burst. Propping himself on his elbows, he tried to drag himself the remaining distance while a T-34 headed straight for him. For a moment he paused, gathering his strength for a last desperate effort. With great presence of mind he allowed the steel monster to approach and, a few metres short, hurled himself aside. Either by grim mischance or due to the alert reactions of the tank driver the vehicle changed course abruptly, the tracks crushed and then entangled the man's legs: the mechanical system drew him into the innards and mangled him to death.

To our bewilderment, having crossed through our positions, the T-34s kept on going instead of turning to sandwich us between Soviet armour and infantry as expected. The only explanation was a break-down in communications or an overestimation of our ability to resist. As the tanks disappeared towards the rearward lines, we geared ourselves to tackle the Russian soldiers of foot, who were rushing our lines shorn of protection.

Snipers – who were both hated and feared – were tortured to death if captured. Accordingly, at every impending attack I decided how I would get rid of my sniper's carbine with its tell-tale telescopic sight should the need arise, and I had prepared a hiding place for it among some ammunition boxes. Shortly before the wave of Russian attackers reached our trenches, I concealed it and took up an MP-40 instead. With a rousing 'Hurrah!' the Reds threw themselves upon our positions and merciless hand-to-hand fighting broke out. Driven by a primeval instinct, we embarked upon an orgy of in-fighting. Here a rifle butt smashed into a face; an MP burst transformed a stomach into a bloody, steaming mass; a shovel edge clove a man's shoulders; bayonets and knives stabbed and ripped. Against a backdrop of death cries, groans, screams, the occasional pistol round, gun-smoke, sweat and blood, we abandoned our humanity.

Like a sack of potatoes, a mortally wounded Russian fell into the trench. His ribs intercepted a bayonet jab from a comrade, which had been intended for me. The bayonet tangled in his body, and the Soviet tugged to free the weapon a second too long. Pushing the first Russian away from me, I let the second have the full force of my iron-capped mountain boot in his testicles. A crack told me that I had split the pubic bone. Screaming, his face contorted with pain, the Russian fell on his back. I fell on him, pressing my thumbs to his windpipe. In response he gurgled, eyes bulging from their sockets. From the corner of my eye I saw a dark shadow lunge at me. Ducking instinctively, my steel helmet took the force of a blow struck with the butt of a rifle. Slightly stunned, I rolled to one side and crossed my arms in front of my face to parry the next jab. A burst of MP-fire raked his back, spattering me with blood and ribbons of intestine. As I jumped up, I saw a Russian bayonet stab into the kidneys of the *Jäger* who had saved me. In terrible agony he froze like a column of salt. The rifle of the dead Russian was at hand and, snatching it swiftly, I rammed the iron-ended stock into the face of the third enemy soldier before he could free his bayonet. Blood seeped from the amorphous mass which had once been his face, and it was an easy job to deliver him the *coup de grâce*.

Amid this raging carnage I lost all sense of time, horror and pity. Shortly before, I had been sprayed in the face with earth when an enemy grenade exploded nearby, and felt a light blow to my nose and jawbone. Only now as the fighting ebbed did I taste the blood and become aware of the sticky mass on my face and neck. A handful of German infantry stood surveying a medieval-like battlefield of groaning, crying, dying and dead soldiers. 'Sepp, you've been hit. Let's have a look at it,' a comrade said. My right nostril had been split and a number of tiny metal splinters had lodged in my lower lip, but there was no time to seek medical aid, for with shouts of 'Hurrah!' the next wave of Russian infantry was approaching from afar. The few of us still able to fight closed ranks. Gathering up the weapons and ammunition of our fallen, we occupied an earth bunker about 200 metres behind the front line. Prudence dictated that I should leave my sniper's rifle behind in its hiding place.

In the ensuing mêlée we succeeded in holding the bunker, but another group was not so fortunate. Twenty *Jäger* had been cut off and were forced to occupy a forward trench, from where they offered stout resistance until their ammunition ran out. The five survivors surrendered to the enemy, and we watched as they were hustled away with kicks and blows from rifle stocks.

The fifteen Russian tanks which had combed through our lines and kept going, came to a sorry end when ambushed by two SP-guns and an 88. This removed the threat to our rear. We received a signal from company that the two SP-guns had been sent forward and on their arrival would launch an immediate counter-attack to tie down Russian forces in the sector for as long as possible.

Both sides were in the process of reorganizing. For the time being I was armed only with a standard K98k rifle without telescopic sight, but even so, using the occasional well-aimed reminder I forced the Russians to keep their distance. In this kind of situation there is no opportunity to camouflage. The sniper seeks out a protected lay with a good field of fire and continues to shoot from this position amid his comrades until spotted and targeted or the battle line changes.

It took an hour for the SP-guns to arrive. An attack plan was quickly decided upon and we moved out. Eighty *Jäger* afforded cover by the SP-guns were to attempt the recapture of our forward trenches. For the moment the Russians had made a tactical error and were not able to reinforce their depleted units. Visibly surprised by the counter-attack, they took to their heels and were soon back in their original positions. I discovered my sniper's rifle undamaged among the ammunition boxes where I had left it.

The impetus of his attack convinced the SP-guns' commander to keep on going for the Russian lines. With my carbine I maintained a rapid, accurate fire aimed at senior enemy personnel, hampering their efforts to assemble some kind of effective defence. Bereft of their tanks and lacking heavy infantry weapons, their line began to crumble piecemeal. As they withdrew further, I attempted to inflict the maximum casualties, and I lost count of the number that fell to my shooting.

When the chance arose, I reported to a dressing station to have my wounds looked at. My nose received stitches and a plaster, the metal splinters in my lip were drawn out using a magnet. The wounds hardly merited a few days of convalescence, and so I remained at the front.

Our attack was driven home with determination and the Soviet defence line began to dissolve. I was assigned to a twelve-man platoon to clear a stretch of enemy positions. We encountered no resistance and found only dead and badly wounded enemy soldiers. However, we remained alert, for there were a number of well-built lower workings that might have concealed an ambush force. Cautiously, and watching to all sides, we approached one of these workings, from inside which issued some gurgling noises. A *Jäger* called out in Russian that anybody inside should come out at once with his hands up, and when nothing happened he fired a burst from his MP-40 into the gloom. Still nothing stirred, although the gurgling noises continued. Gingerly, he felt his way forward. There was a chink in the ceiling which served to throw a pale gleam into the room ahead. Scarcely had he put a foot inside than he cried out in horror. We were confronted by a scene of ghastly cruelty. The five *Jäger* whom we had seen taken away from their trench as prisoners were gurgling in their own blood. The Russians had cut their throats, not wishing to draw attention to their presence by shooting the men instead. Their arms and legs trembled uncontrollably, their hands clawed helplessly at the dirt floor. They were beyond help, but it was an age before death brought an end to their suffering.

It was experiences such as these which made one hard and ruthless towards the Soviets. The question of whether this kind of shot or that was ethical faded into irrelevance when the recipient was this particular enemy. Within me at least, they sowed the seed of a hatred for all of them without exception, and I vowed that I would never spare a single one of them if I had the chance to shoot. It was a phenomenon shared by both sides. Everybody legitimized his behaviour in revenge.

My comrades were none too fussy in this regard. A Russian sergeant who had been left behind because of a leg injury became the scapegoat for the five murdered German infantrymen. They required of him information about positions and assembly points, attack plans and so forth. It was irrelevant to them that the man obviously had very little knowledge regarding such matters, it was simply an excuse to exact revenge. In any case, his replies to the lieutenant and assistants to the inquisition were not satisfactory, even though the occasional punch in the face was thought likely to loosen his tongue a fraction. Even if he knew everything and had spilt the beans, it would still not have been enough; another excuse would have been found. The brutality of the interrogation escalated. Finally one of the assistants decided that sharpened matchsticks should be driven below the fingernails of the prisoner 'to make him talk', and the screams of pain this induced seemed to egg on the torturers. It was a veteran warrant officer who put an end to the scene, saying, 'Enough of this shit, you're as bad as Ivan.' He took his 08 from its holster and shot the Russian in the back of the head. A silence fell and the inquisition at last came to its senses. The lieutenant made no protest at the disrespect shown to his rank: the shot seemed to bring him out of a trance.

While German losses in men and material were never fully made good, the Russians could call upon seemingly bottomless reserves

37

from the hinterland, and on 19 December 1943 they unfolded a fresh offensive against the Nikopol bridgehead. For the purpose they had ten full divisions supported by fighters and bombers unopposed in the air. Like incoming surf, the endless waves of tanks and infantry swept towards the German lines, and after twelve days of unceasing assault, 3.G.D. was virtually wiped out. On some sectors of the front, one or two German infantrymen were asked to defend 100 metres of front under pressure from a force fifty times their number. Even the most battle-hardened veteran was affected by the stress of living in perpetual fear. On the last two days of 1943, elements of G.J.R. 144 began to crack. In the face of this very dangerous development, the regimental adjutant and ordnance officer toured the front line aboard a motor-cycle combination in an attempt to rally spirits and urge the men to hold on.

I was with 7./144, which had held off unceasing attacks for days. Constantly changing my position I loosed off the occasional deadly round to keep the Russians under cover and afford my comrades some respite. By some miracle I continued to survive all bombardments unscathed, aware of our horrifying casualty rate. It was when isolated singly or with only one comrade in a trench complex, the lines of communication and supply having broken down, that panic would suddenly seize the occupants. Anything could be the catalyst: lack of ammunition, the sudden realization that one was totally alone, the loss of contact to the command post, the wounded left untreated, the sight of other trenches being abandoned. Even though I had the invaluable advantage of being at liberty to wander our sector, now and again I felt the almost irresistible impulse to get away from the front line to the relative safety at company HQ.

Whenever I dropped in on a stretch of trench, the relief of the occupants was only too visible. Their garrulous talk and questions as to how things stood where I had just come from had about them the stench of imminent disaster. I found a dugout staffed by a solitary MG-gunner. His nerve had gone. 'Sepp, take me with you,' he begged in despair, 'Shit, they don't come for the wounded any more, and we get no ammunition or food.' At that instant we heard the snarl of an approaching motor-cycle and watched as its *Hauptmann* rider laid the machine on its side and sprinted in a zigzag towards us. His arrival coincided with the decision of five men in a neighbouring trench to give up and head for the rear. Realizing at once that if not nipped in the bud it could start an avalanche, he tore free the MP-40 slung round his neck and fired a burst over their heads. The group paused and turned to stare at the officer. They seemed thunderstruck. Suddenly one of the group raised his rifle and fired, the bullet narrowly missing the captain who retaliated by aiming his machine-pistol at the rebel, lining him up in its sights. 'Weapons down and back in the trench, you scum!' he bawled. The men came to their senses. The officer lowered the MP-40 but kept it ready. As he strode up to the five a Russian mortar bombardment began, forcing everybody low. The officer was in the vacant trench before its former occupants made their scrambled return. Ten minutes later, filthy and exhausted, he arrived at my side as a salvo of light mortars sighed overhead. The three of us, the captain, the MG-gunner and I, watched as they fell long, exploding into the ground, where they threw up a great spray of earth. A few seconds later clumps of turf pattered down around us. The captain exuded a certain confidence which told me that he knew something. 'Men, don't do anything stupid. Just hold out, all is in hand,' he assured us ducking his head as more mortars swept overhead 'The Russians can't keep up this pressure. So far, everyone has held his position in the most exemplary manner. We are in the process of constructing a new defensive line and will soon fall back in good order. The lines of communication will be restored later today. Just hold on. I am relying on you.' With that, and always keeping to cover, he scrambled for the next trench, leaving behind the present of a box of chocolate bars, which we devoured greedily. A half-hour later I changed my position. It was amazing to witness the effect of the staff officer's visit. The German infantrymen held firm. A potentially disastrous and deadly panic had been averted, and the front remained stable.

Of course, not all men could take the stress, and many reported to the field hospital with self-inflicted wounds or feigned illnesses. It was an art in which a number of men specialized, imparting their secret knowledge of techniques only to a select few. I found out that eating Nivea cream brought about symptoms identical to yellow jaundice. To avoid powder traces and burns at the edges of self-inflicted wounds to hand or foot, the round had to be fired through a loaf of black bread. Feigned illness became prevalent before major offensives, under battle-stress of long duration or where general environmental conditions were bad. Even officers and NCOs could succumb in this way, and occasionally segments of the front were left unattended after more senior ranks abandoned their charge, leaving subordinates in the lurch.

Surprised by the degree of bitter resistance they encountered, the Russians finally gave it up as a bad job and transferred the bulk of their force to the north-east, reinforcing an offensive that held out more promise. German reconnaissance had been on the alert for such indications, and the change in objective was quickly spotted. At last the survivors of 7./144 could be withdrawn to the rearward assembly area, acknowledging with satisfaction that Herr *Hauptmann* had stated the truth when he forecast that a new defensive line had been set up.

In temporary safety we lay strewn on the floor of the earth bunker in utter exhaustion, when a medic sergeant aroused us from our stupor. 'Men, here's ink for your fountain pens,' he proclaimed as he passed from one man to another distributing small glass phials of tablets under the label 'Pervitin'. These were metamphetamines, which suppressed hunger and the desire to sleep, increased psychic resistance and induced a slight euphoria. Just what the doctor ordered. 'When you feel run down,' he explained, as though he were addressing a bunch of the over-fifties, 'just pop one of your pills and your inner motor will run a little better. But a word to the wise – don't overdose or you will flake out quicker than you can say Peep and that's the last thing we want, isn't it?' Evidently these pills were the priority, for only after he had finished the distribution and pep-talk did he turn his attention to the wounded being brought in.

After a few hours' comatose sleep we were shaken awake and ordered to take a pill. Afterwards we were served hot coffee and a couple of slugs of schnapps. This mixture was making itself felt by the time we were on the road for the defensive line, and to burn off the worst of our strange mood, after half an hour we were ordered towards the Russian offensive at the double. The men of an infantry division were in urgent need of support, and 7./144 was going to provide it. The only thing was, it meant that we had a very long march ahead of us.

Chapter 4

Retreat from
Nikopol

A thaw had set in and we were obliged to force a way through an often knee-high quagmire. Boots and socks were saturated and then weighted down by thick mud. In total exhaustion, our progress forward was mechanical. It was not uncommon to come across a man who had fallen asleep upright in the place where he had come to a standstill: a comrade would take his hand and drag him onwards. Minutes later he would come fully awake and, in shock, remember nothing. The effort required on this march was so enormous that it virtually defeated the Pervitin tablets. I carried my sniper's rifle slung across my back, the weapon wrapped around by a thick strip of tent cloth to protect it against the mud. My MP-40 dangled across my chest. I had developed the habit of chewing dry biscuits to stave off lethargy – I had a store of them for which I traded my cigarette ration.

More lay behind the Russian manoeuvres than a mere transfer of the weight of their attack strongpoint. Their operation developed into a major offensive which on 30 January 1944 drove a great wedge through the German lines, threatening to double round two German armies at the Basawluk estuary on the great bend in the Dnieper. As was so often the case, the OKH dallied until it was almost too late before ordering an urgent shortening of the front. Our forces were saved only by the incompetence of the Russian commanders who, at the decisive moment, elected to rest and reorganize away from the critical area rather than mass for the crucial thrust to the Dnieper bend. More by luck than judgement therefore, the OKH succeeded in arranging their forces in such a manner that the Russian operation, when it came, ran up against enough resistance to stifle it. And it was to support these positions that we ploughed our way through the mire.

Wearing soaking winter battle gear, hunger and exhaustion etched in our faces, we fought mechanically, ghosts driven only by the personal desire to survive. There were no pauses in the battle any longer. I fell ill. Constant hypothermia combined with drinking the water found in bomb craters resulted in severe gastro-enteritis. During one of his rounds the battalion commander found me curled up like a wounded animal, trembling in the corner of a shelter.

Hauptmann Max Kloss was a dark-haired young officer of slight build who had taken command of the battalion at the Nikopol bridgehead. He had volunteered to transfer to the Russian Front from Lapland in the belief that he would be of greater service to the Reich where soldiers were needed most urgently. He was impregnated with National Socialist values which stated that a thing worth doing was worth doing well, and as an outward expression of his belief he wore the red and white diamond-shaped badge of the Hitler Youth beside the Iron Cross, First Class on the left breast pocket of his uniform tunic. On the other pocket he wore the German Cross in Gold. Yet he was no blindly faithful Party follower, but rather a committed and brave soldier. Seeing my pitiful condition, he requested an explanation from my company commander, who was accompanying him. The latter replied that I was a sniper who knew his business. 'We need every specialist, we've got to get this man on his feet,' Kloss stated firmly, 'he is the last sniper we have left, I cannot afford to lose him.' So saying, he ordered me to report to the battalion command post and associate with the despatch runners. 'Tell them to look after you,' he said, adding, as he turned to the other officer, 'I hope you have no objection, Herr *Oberleutnant?*' The latter shrugged his shoulders. Trembling, I rose and dragged myself off. It was a kilometre, and after a series of toilet stops on the way I arrived at the runners' lodge (a hole excavated into the ground with a roof of logs), threw myself into the sleeping area and groaned, 'The commander says you're supposed to look after me. To start off, if you don't mind, I need new trousers.'

'Certainly, Fräulein Allerberger, the Professor will be along shortly to powder your tender little arse,' one confirmed, but all the same they really did look after me, supplying me with tea without milk and an extremely effective diarrhoea preventive called Dolantin. This was an anti-spasmodic analgesic developed by Hoechst in 1939 and used to suppress the pain from wounds. In the early 1940s, Hoechst chemists succeeded in increasing its effectiveness twenty-fold, the new drug having the name Polamidon. In 1944, Germany produced around 650 tonnes of analgesics.

Dolantin, bedrest and proper nutrition restored me to health within a few days. The nursing care lavished on me by the despatch runners was a tremendous help. The battalion commander visited me occasionally to enquire after my progress and during our talks it emerged that we saw eye-to-eye on many things. On the day I regained mobility, albeit still shaky around the knees, Kloss told me, 'It's high time we got you back to work. There are four new NCOs coming, I have put them with your company, I was thinking you might show them what you know. My driver will take you.'

Fifteen minutes later I was in a *Kübelwagen* spluttering down a dirt track to company. We were less than three minutes out when the left side front wheel hit a landmine. The steering wheel was knocked from the driver's grasp and the vehicle sheered to the left. I heard a cry of 'Shit!' and found myself hurtling through the air alongside the driver, the pair of us making a soft landing in the quagmire skirting the track. The *Kübelwagen* tipped over and came to rest on its side minus a wheel. Neither of us dared move and we remained pressed to the ground. 'That shit thing must have been one of ours,' the driver said, 'yesterday it was mine-free here and Ivan hasn't been near the place for days. Are you hurt?' Apart from a few bruises I had escaped scot-free again. On all fours, feeling our way gingerly forward with our fingertips, we made our way back to the car.

While discussing our next move we saw a column of engineers – *Pioniere* – approaching. 'What are you people doing here?' the corporal cried, 'and who gave you permission to set off our carefully laid mines?' Their gentle cynicism failed to mollify us.

'You assholes are supposed to tell people where you are putting your mines,' the driver retorted.

'Well, now you know,' came the response, 'and if you're rude we'll just leave you here. I suggest that you two gentlemen tag along behind us,' the platoon corporal said, leading off smartly.

'That *Kübelwagen*'s not going anywhere, so we might as well follow,' my driver muttered. The road to company was barriered off, and we were soon back at battalion HQ to deliver our report. The outcome was that Kloss placed me under his direct command and lodged me with the despatch runners. The latter shaved every morning (a ritual I had attempted to observe for some time), lived beyond the direct line of fire, wore clean uniforms and ate regularly, and I considered this a great improvement to living in a trench at company.

The Russians threw everything at us in the attempt to achieve their objective. On the battlefield we wanted to fight by rules and so avoid all-out mayhem. Our attempts to convince the Soviets met with little success: the Soviets set the ground rules from the beginning and repaid our initial success with barbarity. Particularly incomprehensible, however, was their unspeakable bestiality to civilian populations, not only enemy and neutral, but Russian as well.

Despite heavy bombardment, we succeeded in transporting two desperately needed batteries from G.A.R. 112 (Artillery Regiment) into the Nikopol bridgehead by rail. There was an immediate threat of encirclement, and it had been decided to evacuate the seriously wounded. Only one locomotive had survived the incoming endeavour undamaged, and it was to return to the west pulling an ambulance train composed of cattle-trucks painted with the Red Cross on a white background on the side panelling. That morning, when in a platoon marching to our new positions, our route took us past the loading bay. Hundreds of wounded, many wearing only the scantiest field dressings to cover terrible injuries, lay around the wagons. We were appalled at the numbers of dead and horribly mutilated. Upon seeing us, hope revived in the eyes of the moribund. Many made the same plea: 'Hold off Ivan until the train has got clear.' The words struck a chord in the hearts of one or two riflemen, and ignited in them a spark of motivation to do the best they could to comply.

In reality the situation was desperate, for the Soviets had come to within 1,500 metres of the loading bay. Upon leaving the area we came under fire: vastly outnumbered, our resistance amounted to little more than a delaying tactic. Meanwhile the ambulance train had managed to pull away, but the Soviets switched their priority to destroying it by artillery bombardment, and a few minutes later it was strafed and bombed from the air by fighters. The truck carrying the medical personnel received the first direct hit, killing all but two of the surgeons. An explosion derailed the train, the trucks piling into each other at crazy angles, spewing out the wounded in all directions. The magnitude of the disaster was such that the few surviving surgeons and medics were utterly overwhelmed.

We held the front line ahead until the following morning. The route of our withdrawal brought us once more to the ghastly place.

Hanging from the wrecked trucks, limbs in crazy dislocation, were the dead. Arms and legs were strewn across the terrain, their bandages fluttering in the wind. In their panic, most of the wounded had attempted to drag themselves clear on all fours, but the majority lacked strength for the effort, their wounds had reopened and they either bled to death, or their circulatory system collapsed. The radius of the killing field, littered with corpses, extended 300 metres from the train wreck. The handful of medics and doctors had done what they could. Hope grew at our approach: a group of fifty German riflemen, half of them in need of proper medical attention themselves.

The Russians were hot on our heels and would arrive within the hour. We helped by improvising stretchers and agreed on a cruel selection process, picking out those still able to walk or who had a realistic chance of surviving a stretcher journey. The remainder would be left behind. Twenty-four hours previously we had to some extent envied the wounded, since at least theoretically they had come through and were now headed for home, but now the war had seized them back, restored them to our ranks and given them the task of fighting for their lives should they wish to continue living.

A pistol shot rang out. Instinctively all looked towards the report. A *Jäger*, 08 in his hand, was standing over the body of one of the wounded. I strode over and asked the man, 'What the hell have you done?' With a sob he sank to his knees, and it was a few minutes before he composed himself enough to reply. I looked at the body of his friend and neighbour, both legs amputated, the stumps ripped apart and bleeding, the upper torso riddled with steel splinters. It was incredible that he had survived so long with such injuries. The man knew he would be left behind to fall into Russian hands. When the two friends met, he had pleaded for a last act of friendship – a bullet to bring his suffering to an end. He implored so passionately that his friend fulfilled his request. This kind of thing was absolutely contrary to regulations. As we trudged away from the grim location, we hoped that the Russians, when they arrived, would care for the wounded or at least put them swiftly out of their misery. It was an awful lot to expect. Often they tortured the wounded, and had there been no surgeons present, very possibly we would have performed a kindness for all the living we had to leave behind.

I prepared my sniper's rifle and brought up the rear about 500 metres behind the main group. We had been no more than thirty minutes on the march when I became aware of a Russian assault troop not far behind. I concealed myself amongst undergrowth, and rested the barrel of my rifle on the thick forked branch of a tree. My field of fire was obstructed by bushes which the Russians used skilfully for cover. Routine, intuition and the feel for a situation inbred in the born hunter paid off in such situations. At 150 metres I identified the platoon leader, lined the crosswires of the telescopic sight at his chest and watched his passage through the dense vegetation. The right moment came. For a second or so he was exposed between bushes. I squeezed the trigger and saw the impact of the projectile hurtle him backwards into the brush. His platoon was sufficiently astute to recognize the work of a sniper, and sprayed out in all directions for cover. I got off two more rounds without definite result, although one hit a field flask and kept all of them low for the next half hour, gaining precious time for my retreating group. Once I rejoined them to report my success, a number of riflemen volunteered to protect the rear of our column with me, and to my surprise by evening we had remained undetected. During the night our path coincided with that of another *Jäger* battalion. This provided us with a formation of respectable numbers and we soon received a signal ordering us to dig in and stem the Russian advance for as long as possible.

A sharpshooter whom I knew only by repute was Josef Roth, a Nuremberger of my own age who had volunteered for the *Gebirgsjäger*, and on his own initiative practised with a captured Russian rifle, as I had done, and found employment as a sniper. I sought him out from among the other battalion and we got on handsomely from the start. The battalion commander knew how important it was to have snipers integrated into the defensive pattern and allowed us a free hand. While the other riflemen dug trenches, Josef and I carried out a joint reconnaissance of the terrain and then settled down to work out our plan. We agreed that two experts working as a pair were better than marksmen operating singly.

For three days the weather had been dry, with temperatures slightly above freezing. Towards eight next morning, a shot whipped into the trench-diggers. A private soldier crumpled up, screaming. Like greased lightning the others all threw themselves to the ground, bar one, who dithered a split second, debating whether he should help his fallen friend. He would never have heard the bullet which entered his skull behind the left ear and exited through the right eye, leaving a hole the size of a fist. Somebody yelled, '*Achtung*, snipers!'

From their sentinel nests the MG-gunners poured streams of fire in the general direction of the presumed sniper, but without apparent effect.

Josef and I were still discussing our arrangements at battalion command when a breathless despatch runner arrived to blurt out his report of events. The commander looked up: 'Well *Jäger*, you know your duty, solve the problem.' At a trot, keeping carefully to cover, we followed the runner to a recently finished stretch of trench where a sergeant elaborated the details. A shallow gallery led from one end of the trench into a skilfully concealed observation post amongst a clump of bushes. From this lookout position we scrutinized the terrain for all possible sniper hides, but failed to identify a spot even though we were suspicious of one particular region because it matched the angle of fire at the end of which our two comrades had been felled. We kept a watch in vain for hours. Josef said there was no position opposite that looked remotely ideal. At midday, while emptying a fruit tin of excrement over the trench parapet, a third *Jäger* fell victim to the Russian marksman: he was somewhat luckier twice over than the other two, however, for the projectile was deflected from the rim of his steel helmet into his upper arm where it opened a gaping wound only. Contrary to practice, the Russian had not used an explosive bullet. At that very moment, Josef and I were observing the enemy front line through binoculars. We both noticed how the tall grass fronting a low undulation parted briefly under the pressure wave of the shot. We had to admire the ingenuity of our opponent in creating such a neat lair: he must have burrowed through the elevation from the back. The question was, did he have enough experience to abandon the position, or would he stay? The latter seemed more likely, since all three of our victims had been hit from roughly the same direction. We had to get him to show himself, and decided on the use of a lure. Josef would take up a position about 50 metres along the trench while I remained in the observation post: we would aim and fire simultaneously at the spot where the grass moved. A scarecrow dressed in camouflage jacket and peaked field cap was prepared, and while sneaking to his position Josef handed the scarecrow to a rifleman halfway along with the instruction that in exactly ten minutes' time it was to be raised cautiously until the field cap was visible above the parapet.

Our two rifles were focused on the presumed hide of the Russian sniper, waiting for the scarecrow to make his debut. When it rose, the

Soviet made his fatal error. He was over-confident, and that was what killed him. Clearly he had already dismissed from his mind the idea of a lure, and was therefore not even certain of his target when he fired from an unchanged position. Hardly had his shot rung out than we replied, each using one of our precious captured explosive rounds. I watched the drama through the sight: a flurry of hectic activity and then something heavy being dragged away. A Soviet observer offered himself for death by standing up and surveying our lines through binoculars. Both bullets drilled into his head simultaneously, exploding it like an overripe pumpkin. His binoculars dropped to his chest undamaged. Now it was the turn of the Russians to cower in their dugouts, enabling our diggers to resume their excavations.

Branching forward from our front line at various distances along its length were shallow communication trenches leading to a pair of MG nests. Josef and I designed and dug six well-camouflaged hides, three each, the most forward locations being situated between each MG position. This allowed us to cover No-Man's-Land in such a way that no area was obscured from our field of fire. Our plan was to keep up a lethal crossfire until the advancing Russian infantry was at 100 metres, then change to shooting directly ahead. Further down each branch were two more rearward positions for the contingency that we were spotted. This strategy worked and was a major contributory factor towards the success of our battalion in holding off the Russian attack for two days, during which time we evacuated our wounded, including the survivors from the ambulance train.

The pressure on the Nikopol bridgehead was soon irresistible and a new encirclement began to threaten. The merged battalions were parted in the general reorganization. Josef and I shook hands and expressed the hope that we would meet in the future under happier circumstances. Our cooperation had proved that having a specialist observer alongside could be a decisive factor. Although after the death of Balduin Moser I had vowed to work alone, I saw that teamwork had definite advantages, a fact of which I managed to convince my company commander to the extent that he assented to my recruiting a veteran helper whenever I considered the opportunity favourable.

Our two regiments began their bitter struggle to escape the Russian encircling manoeuvre. G.J.R. 144 was assigned the role of mounting diversionary raids aimed at keeping open important crossroads to be used by our retreating forces. Our numbers severely reduced, it was close to miraculous that we kept the line intact, and even launched the odd counter-attack to give a deceptive impression of our strength. We suffered grievous losses, and the continued existence of our weakened regiment was never guaranteed, for whole companies were wiped out to the last man.

On 12 February 1944, after four days of bitter fighting, the order came down to evacuate the Nikopol bridgehead. By now our regiment had been so long without supplies that we lacked heavy infantry weapons altogether and every rifleman had a maximum of ten rounds. Since we were under continuous pressure from the enemy the situation was extremely grave, and the few snipers were called upon to serve the role of 'the artillery'. We were the last desperate line of defence, the last hope of holding the Soviets at a distance, and every man went to work gathering together all available Russian rifle ammunition.

3.G.D. fought out of the encirclement after great effort and with heavy losses, and reached the new front line at Ingulez. We were assisted by severe winter weather, ice and snowstorms, which made organized fighting impossible, but did nothing to alleviate our weakened state. In apathy we staggered across the flat steppe, ice crystals adhering to pinched features like needles. The Celsius thermometer read 50 below zero. Whoever stopped moving or fell in exhaustion had deadly frostbite within minutes. The hob-nailed soles of our mountain boots were a conduit for the cold: if one had sweaty socks often the skin would freeze to the boot, and then the wearer could only creep forward. The medics could do nothing to help because all liquid medications were frozen in their containers, although for the worst cases they always kept some morphine ampoules available in their mouths. Wounds froze at once and became gangrenous: fights broke out for possession of winter clothing found on stiff-frozen Russian corpses: happy the man who emerged wealthier by a snow hat or fur boots.

Remorselessly the battalion pressed on. On occasion when I stopped for a breather, I received encouragement to proceed by a kick in the rear or a prod with a rifle butt, and when necessary I repaid the compliment. Many of our number died of the cold or total exhaustion, reducing ever lower our number of fighting fit. We dragged the wounded along with us so long as any individual retained a prospect of recovery, otherwise they were abandoned, together with the mules that could go no further, having long since consumed the last of their oats. Our ice-coated weapons were useless. The extreme cold contracted the steel to jam the breeches. The expensive precision work, which was the hallmark of the German weapons manufacturer, was now a curse: Russian weapons with their much greater tolerances functioned even in the lowest temperatures. Trench digging in the stone-hard ground was out of the question. Driven on by the instinct to survive, we dragged our way through the pitiless steppe as the snowstorm grew in intensity. Numb from hunger and exhaustion, I staggered through the knee-high snow, my sniper's rifle slung across my back and wrapped in a thick blanket for protection. Over my uniform I wore a padded camouflage jacket, the large hood covering my head and face.

After a while there emerged through the impenetrable greyness of the storm the silhouette of a gutted farmhouse with a giant haystack alongside it. By now the cold was almost intolerable. As I turned towards it, the ground gave way. With a cry I fell into an infantry trench. One of the occupants was still present, stiff as a board, a smile frozen across his features. Like a wild beetle I scrambled on all fours to the surface. The farmhouse was only 30 metres distant. Suddenly movement was seen from within it, and we spread out quickly. My limbs were so cold that I could not unburden myself of the rifle: various gyrations proved unsuccessful. We were defenceless. Scraps of Russian conversation were borne to us on the wind. Fearfully, we awaited the bursts of MG-fire that would spell our doom. Nothing happened. Minutes of terrible uncertainty ticked by until it was obvious: the Russians were snowbound and unable to fight. Both sides withdrew gingerly. Night came, and the storm grew fiercer. Getting under cover now meant the difference between life and death. We slunk towards the giant haystack, the only protection far and wide against the rage of nature. We had reached the point where nobody cared any more. Shelter was all that mattered. We ran the last few metres and burrowed deeply into the warming straw. Abandoning all rules of self-protection and security, we huddled together like piglets and so survived. During the two days and nights when it raged with unrestrained fury, we suspended hostilities, for the haystack was the only chance of survival for the Russians as well. Unable to fight, the respective bitter enemies agreed to share the stack, separated by a central demarcation line.

The storm abated on the morning of 20 February 1944 by which time our weapons were again serviceable. Nervously we reconnoitred

1. Allerberger and a Selbstladegewehr (self-loading rifle) Modell 43 with telescopic sight, 20 April 1945. This semi-automatic carbine was a very favourable advance with some of the recoil energy when fired being diverted to the reloading function.

2. *Obergefreiter* Josef Sepp Allerberger

3. The concept: a *Wehrmach[t]* propaganda photo of a *Gebirgsjäger* sniper.

4. Most successful *Wehrmacht* sniper *Obergefreiter* Mathias Hetzenauer was also attached to 3.G.D. The weapon he holds is the K98k standard carbine with side mounted Zeiss Zielsechs telescopic sight.

the giant haystack, feeling cautiously for the Russians. They had decided that discretion was the better part of valour and vanished into the night. A three-man patrol, waist-high in snow, inspected the farmhouse for signs of life. They came back relieved – we had the farm to ourselves.

Shortly afterwards we resumed our trudge across the endless, deathly-still desert of snow towards the new strongpoint at Ingulez. We had not eaten for days and were close to collapse, when we stumbled into a ruined village held by our troops from whom our regiment obtained ammunition, clothing, blankets and food. As I was attached to battalion staff, I wallowed in the luxury of superior accommodation (in so far as there was such a thing), equipped with an oven. I was dozing in a cosy corner when *Hauptmann* Kloss returned from a regimental briefing. Trembling with cold he crouched before the roaring fire of the stove, then thrust his soaked boots close to the warmth. A pleasant feeling of relaxation must have crept over him, for he slumped back against the wall and was soon asleep. A short while later when I happened to glance in his direction I noticed smoke rising from his boots. Within a few moments he jumped up with a cry of, 'Shit! That's hot!' and began to hop around the room. His efforts to pull off the boots, though assisted by a runner, were unsuccessful. The wet leather had dried too quickly in the heat and, shrinking, had moulded to his feet. The only remedy was for Kloss to sit with the boots immersed in a bucket of cold water and wait for the leather to soften and expand. To wide grins from a large assembly, the crisis was eventually overcome. Later that day a new uniform issue was announced, and Kloss was able to exchange his leather boots for a fur-lined pair.

On 25 February 1944 the Russians attacked but were repulsed by the defensive barrage of a newly operational mountain artillery regiment. Meanwhile the infantry fell back on Ingulez, where the new front line had been established. As so often in the past it had been bungled. While officers on the spot had planned correctly for the strategic and tactical situation, OKH intervened to order the holding of utterly superfluous positions at all costs. The result was more heavy losses in men and materials, neither of which were now capable of being made good, for logistically it was no longer possible to compensate the huge drain on resources on this front even though the lines of communication were regularly shrinking in length. The military operation degenerated into a chaotic struggle to retreat in which the watchword was '*sauve qui peut*'.

The line at Ingulez was a catastrophe waiting to happen. Requests to shorten the line were refused, the essential reorganization of forces waved brusquely aside. An overstretched and ragged front line awaited Russian attacks, which were ever more gigantic. Divisions and regiments with high morale and extensive experience such as 3.G.D. carried the hopes of local commanders. Repeatedly thrown into the thick of the fray, on their shoulders alone often rested the responsibility of preventing a major breach of the line and the spectre of encirclement. They had no operational security, for whatever lay to the rear was improvised. The price was insufferable losses in men and materials.

Chapter 5

More Horrors on the Road to Ingulez

On 1 March 1944 great waves of Russian foot soldiers streamed towards the German lines. Their determination on this occasion was of especial note. 3.G.D. shared the sector with 1.Pz.Gren.Div. and along this stretch the Soviets made up their losses in personnel daily, with endless marching columns of men arriving from deep in the interior. They lost a thousand men per day, while our losses were nowhere near that figure. On the third day the panzer-grenadiers were wiped out, and we had to plug the gap on the flank. By the fourth day, 3.G.D. had shrunk to half its starting numbers, 50 per cent having fallen in the field or been wounded and unable to continue. Although right in the centre of the fighting, I received no more than a few scratches. Once more, high morale and experience proved for some time that it could compensate for what was sadly lacking in numbers, but by the end of the fifth day, my battalion was reduced to sixty.

While we had been holding at bay an enemy attacking along two sides of the wedge, the sound of violent combat swelled up to our rear, and simultaneously a radio operator received a signal from battalion HQ that they were under heavy attack and were asking for help. An enemy unit had infiltrated behind our lines and was attempting to eradicate our command centre; thirty defenders were outnumbered three-to-one. A violent engagement had begun, and the defenders were now low on ammunition. The battalion HQ structure was not intended as a fortification and casualties were already serious. The main Russian attack on the front line was concentrated further down so that the company commander decided to chance weakening the sector by releasing a couple of men to support the defence of battalion HQ. This was agreed with other company commanders, who also detached a few men each. Soon the necessary battle-proven platoon had been assembled, twenty of us in all, including myself and a specially chosen observer.

The report from battalion HQ had arrived at about eight in the morning: barely an hour later the relief platoon set off to cover the intervening 1,500 metres as quickly as possible but with due caution, and in a quarter of an hour established contact with the enemy. Battalion HQ was set in a depression at the foot of an imposing hill, the terrain being in the main bushy upland. We did not have the strength to hold the hill, but for the Russians it was of strategic importance since from the peak they could overlook the German positions. The defenders had withdrawn to the last remaining fortification and were almost out of ammunition. In response to the withering fire of the Russians, they replied with the occasional rifle round. The area surrounding battalion HQ was strewn with the dead of both sides.

We halted briefly to take stock. With my observer I sought out some thick vegetation which appeared to offer excellent natural cover and a relatively good view of the proceedings. As the platoon settled in, waiting for the signal to attack, my observer sized up the Russian force. Through his binoculars, he had a very wide field of sight in comparison with that available to me through my telescopic sight, and this was bound to help me raise my score of kills significantly by precise indications of where to aim. I watched as an apparently dead German infantryman with a profusely bleeding head wound tried to push himself up with his hands and was immediately cut down by a burst of Russian MG-fire. His head turned into a red mass under the rain of projectiles. 'Small wall of earth, ten metres right,' my observer muttered. Moving my rifle, I soon had the Russian in the sight, aimed at his chest, squeezed the trigger ... bang ... dead. Perfect shot at 150 metres.

This success was the signal to attack. The platoon opened fire. My own projectiles began to eat into the enemy numbers. The skirmish was short and violent. Caught in the unexpected crossfire of platoon and sniper, and horrified by their escalating losses, the Russians lost their heads. Shooting wildly in all directions they withdrew in disorder. Twenty made it into the undergrowth: they left eighty dead and wounded behind. There was no time for anything more: after a short discussion with the battalion HQ survivors we headed once again for the front. Twenty minutes later we were in our own trenches.

The battle raged for six days almost without pause. Towards its conclusion we were so exhausted that it was easy to fall into a coma-like sleep during the shortest period of inactivity. The medics made regular distributions of Pervitin to keep us alert.

3.G.D. held its positions until 7 March 1944 even though the Soviets crossed the Ingulez river the previous day and dynamited parts of the front line. The division became a thorn in their side: to remove us, the usual infantry solution was adopted once more. G.J.R. 144 was at the heart of this pressure: when it got too hot for us we fell back on the regimental HQ and fought there. The command structure had ceased to function. Each group fought for itself, and to survive. During this utter confusion, the order came to retreat across the Ingulez forthwith.

This was easier said than done. The Russians had more or less succeeded in isolating 3.G.D. Its line of supply no longer existed and the main field hospital was in Soviet hands. All that remained was a defended corridor about one kilometre in width through which the retreat had to be funnelled. These were the circumstances under which the few fighting fit survivors and walking wounded of G.J.R. 144 embarked upon their withdrawal, their numbers swollen from time to time by remnants from other units.

Some of the latter included four medics who had fled the Russian assault on the main field hospital. The men were in a highly agitated state and appeared close to mental breakdown, a sign of some terrible experience. A sergeant who asked of them the whys and wherefores received such irrational garble in reply that he shrugged his shoulders in bemusement and passed them to the dressing station with orders that they should be given a meal and a shot of rum. This did the trick, and after a while they were sufficiently calm to be able to deliver an account of their chilling ordeal. We shrank in horror at what they had to tell us, and heightened our will to resist Russian captivity.

Not all the wounded had been allocated a berth on the ill-fated last ambulance train out of the partial encirclement. The hopeless cases had been left behind at the main field hospital under the care of a doctor and seven medics. In order to indicate that the area was *hors de combat*, it had been staked out with Red Cross and white flags, and all weapons placed in the open. It was a Mongolian unit that captured the field hospital. After moving warily from tent to tent they surrounded the area and called upon 'the Fascist swine'

55

inside to come out with their hands raised. The Mongols approached the medical staff nervously, weapons at the ready. Two medics emerged from the surgical operation tent. They had learnt off by heart a few sentences from a Russian phrase book for soldiers on the Eastern Front and said: 'We are unarmed. Here only wounded. We surrender to the Soviet Army.' Hands above the head, the two medics, trembling with fear, awaited the confrontation with the Asiatic soldiers.

The first came up to them and issued an order that was not understood. Immediately the Mongol rammed the stock of his machine-pistol into the face of the medic, breaking his nose. Blood coursed swiftly from between his fingers, which were covering the injury to his mouth. He collapsed to the ground. The Mongol took a step back and fired a burst from his weapon into the upper torso of the injured man. At that moment the surgeon, still wearing a blood-smeared apron, emerged from the operating tent together with an assistant to find out what was going on. Four other Russians arrived, attracted by the commotion, and forced the three Germans back into the operating tent at gunpoint, screaming a series of incomprehensible orders. On the operating table lay a soldier with severe head wounds, which were being bandaged by a fourth medic. One of the Russians pushed past, drew a knife from its scabbard on his belt and drove it into the heart of the patient through his rib-cage, turned it two or three times before withdrawal and made the observation, 'This Fascist pig is no longer required.' The Germans looked on with shock, realizing full well what danger they now found themselves in.

They were forced into an adjoining tent in which the other seriously wounded had been prepared for surgery. A Mongol sergeant pushed the surgeon aside as he pleaded with the Soviet to spare the wounded. The sergeant said, 'Now we will show you what happens to people who invade Mother Russia and kill women and children.' With a gesture to a subordinate he indicated to the wounded men and said, 'Cut their throats like sheep.' Wherever these people came from they must have been expert sheep farmers and slaughterers, for they drew knives, honed to a fine sharpness, from inside their boots and set about the task in hand with great dexterity. Without the least sign of emotion or excitement they raised each head and made a deep incision across the throat. The Mongols worked swiftly and expertly, and in a few minutes the operating theatre had been transformed into

56

a human slaughterhouse. The majority did not die instantly, but bled to death where they lay. The surgeon, who confronted every day the ugliness of war, blanched and collapsed to his knees. 'Weakling!' the Mongol sergeant said, smashing the stock of his machine-pistol in the surgeon's face. Adding, 'You pig, suck my boots', he raised the weapon by the barrel and brought it down with full force on the German's skull. Three similar blows followed to ensure death. The medics were frozen in horror in one corner of the tent. The Mongol pulled one of them to him and wiped the blood-smeared butt of the MP on his uniform.

Since there were no wounded left alive in the hospital, it now occurred to the Russians to loot it. The six surviving medics were forced to sit in front of the operation tent with arms covering their heads guarded by a single Mongol soldier whose irritation at being excluded from the plunder was fairly evident. 'Shit, damn, why have I got to stay here and look after these stupid pigs, can I just shoot them?' he asked the sergeant.

'Shut your mouth and do what I told you,' the sergeant retorted, 'The Old Man wants to have a word with them. Perhaps we can make them sing and tell us where their heroic comrades have hidden supplies.'

One of the German medics understood Russian. 'They are going to finish us off like they did with the wounded,' he whispered. 'We've had it in any case. At the next opportunity I suggest we make a fight of it and run. Our people can't be too far away.'

His comrade nodded. 'OK, I'll kill the Ivan, then we'll run through the operation tent, jump over the amputations trench and then dive into the bushes. We'll keep running until we're safe, each man looks out for himself but tries to keep contact with the others.'

The Russians could be heard admiring their booty in loud tones, especially when they found the food store. The Mongol sentry was by now in a passioned torment and had begun to make urgent requests to his comrades to set aside his share. This was the opportunity. The Russians were rummaging through crates and boxes, the sentry watched them in annoyance and was derelict in his task. In a lightning movement the medic drew a knife from his boot, sprang for his man like a tiger, grabbed the steel helmet by the forward rim, yanked it back into his neck and, throttling the man with the chin-strap, removed him from view of his comrades. A second later with expert anatomical knowledge, the knife went into his right kidney where it was turned in the wound three times for maximum effect. The Russian froze with the sudden terrible pain. The medic suppressed the man's groans by placing a hand over his mouth while lowering him to the ground. To finish the job he should have cut the sentry's throat. His omission was to cost two more German lives, including his own. The German medics now darted through the long tent. They had not quite reached the far end when the death croak of the Mongol sentry reached the ears of his comrades. Several sprays of MP-fire tore through the sailcloth of the tent. The last medic, bloody knife still in his hand, was hit and fell. The others kept running, leapt the open amputations trench, but the fifth caught his foot in a tent line and fell into the trench, stacked high with arms and legs. The fourth had made it to the other side, hesitated, and reached his hand towards the fifth man. As the latter rose, a burst of MP-fire caught him in the back. The four survivors made the adjacent bushes and escaped, the hail of bullets fired into the thick vegetation all missed.

Veterans always carried with them a small hand compass, and one of the medics had one, which saved their lives. It took them two days to hunt down the retreating German forces and elude the enemy. After reporting the names of the dead to the commanding officer, they took their place within the marching column, alone with the memory of their recent harrowing experience.

We had not eaten for days, we were filthy, flea-ridden and at the end of our physical endurance. Arriving at the new battle line we received a briefing. The division was all but out of small arms ammunition. Everybody had to consider very carefully whether he needed to fire at any particular moment. Only the strictest self-discipline and composure would see us through in the coming battles. The alternative was the certainty that the front would crumble, and that meant death in Russian captivity. The private soldier needed to know no more. The German front line had developed into a bulge which the Soviets were proposing to tie off rather like a sack. German 6.Army commanders were engaged in a last-ditch effort to stave off the threatened encirclement. However, had it not been for the lack of coordination between the various Russian armies, the pincer movement could not have been stopped. Fifteen German divisions were now concentrated into a wedge. Their purpose was to break out, cross the Ingulez river, keep going for the Bug river, cross to the west bank and dig in. 3.G.D. had been chosen to spearhead this operation. It was first to the

Ingulez and found a suitable crossing point. A battalion of sappers installed a portable dam while Soviet attacks were disjointed and easily withstood. Meanwhile, advance units of G.J.R. 138 and 144 occupied bridgeheads to secure the crossing and fight off any enemy response. On 15 March 1944, heavy rains preceded strong winds with violent hail and later a blizzard. Without proper shelter, and lacking any hope of medical treatment, the advance guard huddled together in their holes in the ground, feverish and shivering.

It was in low spirits that our motley unit plodded towards the bridgehead alongside columns of 3.G.D. vehicles. The size of the evacuation lent a feeling of security. At the approach to the Ingulez, I saw through intense hail the two regimental commanders in discussion with their staffs about how to defend the crossing point. I was approaching to report my presence when, while still about 30 metres away, there came a warning shout: '*Achtung*! Ivan! Tank!' At that moment a T-34 became dimly visible and opened fire with its MGs. A horse was hit and began to whinny pitifully while our troops dispersed and sprinted for cover. An SP-gun attempted to manoeuvre into position to return fire. The horse was the personal mount of *Oberst* Graf von der Goltz, regimental commander G.J.R. 138. The animal had a gaping wound in the hindquarters. Instead of seeking cover, the *Oberst* went to his horse. Some of the regimental staff officers had thrown themselves to the ground as the tank turret swivelled to take them under fire. Flames leapt from the muzzle of the beast's main gun and the shell, narrowly missing the prostrate officers, turned a group of vehicles into a heap of twisted and burning metal. Metal splinters hummed and whistled through the air; the belly of the horse was ripped wide open; the *Oberst* fell as if hit by an unseen iron fist. The German SP-gun fired at the tank and hit the turret. There was a dull explosion and the T-34 burst into flame. The occupants were probably fried, for they made no attempt to escape. Within minutes the danger had passed. I saw the *Oberst* struggle to his feet. His right arm was gone, except for a jagged piece of bone jutting from the socket. Dumbstruck and in panic he stared at the injury for a few seconds before collapsing unconscious. Then help came running.

For me it was simply another episode in everyday life, but for the division it was a serious loss. Von der Goltz had been an outstandingly competent leader of men and personally brave. An unconventional officer who throughout his career had been continually at odds with his superiors, with the *Gebirgsjäger* he had finally discovered the kind of leadership he could live with and the opportunity to develop his abilities to the full. He was also the only 3.G.D. commander who wore the Oak Leaves. After a few days I learnt that the *Oberst* had died of gangrene in a military hospital at Odessa.

On 16 March 1944 the Russians intensified their pressure on the bridgeheads held by G.J.R. 138 and 144. The fighting was hectic but the defenders held out. 3.G.D. was one of the last divisions across the Ingulez, the tail of the withdrawal being covered by a small rearguard. Here the sniper could come into his own, holding reconnaissance platoons and infantry battle units at a suitable distance while obtaining valuable information about the enemy.

During this stage of the retreat to the Bug river our divisions were very vulnerable, and it was essential to keep the enemy undecided as to our true intentions for as long as possible. The purpose of the rearguard was to offer delaying tactics until the bulk of the main force had reached its new position. To deliberately remain in contact with the enemy, to influence his decisions and movements in this manner required a great deal of discipline and heart, and only the veteran MG-gunner or sniper could be relied upon for the kind of precision work required. Without doubt the sniper provided the most effective form of rearguard. In his disguised hide he awaited the cautiously advancing enemy unit, observed its strength and equipment then forced it to ground with two or three rounds of rapid accurate fire bearing the hallmark of the sniper. This was often sufficient to stop advancing infantry in their tracks for hours at a time.

During the Ingulez retreat the German units moved out at night. I remained behind in one of several carefully prepared positions that were not only well hidden, but provided some security against the effects of shelling. The important thing was that they should offer me the opportunity to make a fast escape unseen. If possible I looked for suitable places in No-Man's-Land so that our own trenches and foxholes were included in my general scheme. When I abandoned the area I left behind booby traps made of hand-grenades and trip-wires. Here the idea was to sow confusion among the enemy during his advance, forcing him to withdraw or present me with a couple of inviting targets for effect.

The sport of resistance and withdrawal went on for four days. Each day I noticed how the Russians had become a little more cautious. In the end I would only manage one or two successful hits daily, for most of them went to earth and stayed there. They became expert at using cover, their preoccupation being to assume total invisibility. My first opportunity for a precise shot had been about 100 metres from my hide, probably an observer who had settled behind some bushes, but betrayed his position by moving incautiously. I noticed the unnatural movement of the leaves and on scrutiny through the telescopic sight made out his silhouette. I aimed at its centre. The hectic trembling of the bush twigs confirmed a hit. I waited on tenterhooks to see what the Russians did next. Nothing. All quiet on the Ingulez front. After an hour I became jittery. Something was not right here. Intently I surveyed No-Man's-Land through binoculars but found no sign of life. My muscles ached and I felt the need for a stretch and crossed my legs. I had just laid my right foot on the left heel when I heard a rifle shot from the Russian side and felt a heavy blow to my right heel. I curled up instinctively deep in my foxhole to examine my painful injury. The entire heel had been shot off the boot and a trail of blood was oozing over the sole. I recognized at once the handiwork of a sniper, and he must have been the best, both by his observation work and marksmanship. It had been a masterly shot. Now my own thought was survival. Since my hide had been identified, I could not afford to reveal an inch of myself, and remained low. For the moment it seemed that the Russian was uncertain. He had no knowledge about the effect of his bullet, and so we had a stand-off. Nobody on the Soviet side was prepared to risk showing himself, and my closest examination of the terrain revealed no trace of my opponent. My hope was that the latter would lie low until the fall of darkness, when I could withdraw unseen. The hours dragged until eventually the onset of night freed me from the trap. I found the exit path I had markered towards the neighbouring company's sector. Next day I remained particularly alert, but luckily my path did not again cross that of my Russian counterpart. A couple of days later the rearguard reached the Bug river and crossed to the west bank unseen.

Our installations on the river bank were solid and of good quality, having been set up two years earlier during the days of our eastward advance, and little extra work had been required to make them 'comfortable'. Meanwhile the Russians surprised us by leaving us entirely to our own devices and we spent a whole week not only recuperating, but rearming and re-equipping. Even some reserves came up. It was like being on holiday. We slept eight hours per day, had regular meals and the occasional shower. But the idyll was short-lived.

On the night of 26 March 1944, using the cover of darkness, Russian assault troops crossed the Bug unobserved and set up a bridgehead below the cliff where battalion II./144 was quartered. At first light, the band of toughened veterans stole into the trenches and overcame the sentries with knives and sharpened entrenching tools. No shots were fired, no prisoners taken. The day was saved by an alert MG-gunner. Observing the opposite bank 200 metres away through binoculars, he noticed a kind of raft or float being let down into the water, and quickly checked the German positions. Glimpsing for a fraction of a second the tops of two Russian helmets above the trench parapet, he raised the alarm.

Shooting broke out, MPs stuttered, cries were heard. The Russian raid had been detected at last, and violent hand-to-hand fighting started in the trenches. In seconds the German defenders were wide awake, armed and manning their positions. The Soviets had embarked upon an amphibious crossing of the Bug, mindless of the murderous defensive fire. Since they had neglected to bring up a single artillery piece to cover them, relying entirely on the element of surprise, we held all the trumps and the invasion from the river was soon in serious difficulties. However, a dangerous situation was developing in the trenches, which we had begun to lose piecemeal section by section. A group had been formed to repulse the infiltration, and this had been partially successful, but the Russians were hanging on to what they had captured, as if their lives depended on it. I was picking off Russians in the boats one by one when an NCO, watching the fighting in the trenches through field glasses, drew my attention to a soldier wearing a white fur cap, apparently the group commander, who was continually seen in the midst of the fighting and seemed to be animating the fierce Russian resistance. 'I think the fine fur cap over there is the leader. If you can knock him out, our people can finish the rest off.' I knew how an officer leading his men in the thick of things could motivate people to fight, and the demoralizing effect when he fell. With a couple of strides I reached a bend in the trench complex from where I had a good field of fire and a place to rest my rifle. With regard to the importance of the task in hand I decided to expend one of my precious explosive rounds. These were found only rarely in captured ammunition. I prepared the weapon and awaited my chance for the fatal shot. The NCO was my observer, watching the opposite trench through his binoculars. Suddenly the fur cap appeared above the trench parapet. 'There, Sepp, to the right!' the NCO yelled. I swung the weapon, but the target had already disappeared. 'Sepp, he's making to the right, wait a bit and you'll see the cap appear above the trench.' I had worked out the rhythm of my opponent. He would soon pass across the sapper's entrance giving me a split second to shoot him. I aimed the crosswires of the sight on the entrance at head height and awaited the decisive moment. Suddenly, 120 metres distant, the target head filled the sight, my shot rang out and hit. Through our respective optics, the NCO and I saw the white fur cap swell like a balloon, then burst like an overripe water melon.

Deprived of their commander, the Russians appeared at once confused and disoriented. Our own assault force used the opportunity to storm the occupied trenches. In the ensuing fighting, the veteran invaders were wiped out to the last man.

I returned my attentions to the river-borne invasion force immediately, and my observer had taken up his carbine. The value of the sniper lies in his ability to distribute a rapid and very accurate fire. The infantry aboard the boats and floats, recognizing that they posed an easy target from the shore, had disembarked very early from the craft in the effort to escape the withering fire. Firing at the heads in the water was just target practice for the sniper. The Russians gave no heed to casualties and the water was red with their blood, rather like the waste drain at a slaughterhouse. A bloody broth of corpses, limbs and internal body organs drifted gently down the stream towards the Black Sea.

A neighbouring sector of the line was captured by the Soviets, but despite the exposed flank G.J.R. 144 repelled everything the Russians could throw at it and held its trenches until 27 March 1944, when 3.G.D. was ordered to retire to the Dniester, 300 kilometres to the south-west. This involved a forty-eight hour enforced march to get clear of the area, but the Russians were wise to it, having learnt their First World War lessons well, and kept on our heels. To add to our problems, the supply line had been severed and we received no ammunition, provisions and, worst of all, no anti-tank weapons. The last lorry to get through brought 2 tonnes of bitter chocolate and 500 Iron Crosses. This kind of administrative lunacy drove us to despair. The daily fare was now half a bar of bitter chocolate and a ship's biscuit, rich in ballast and very good for those vulnerable to loose motions. The two days' forced march failed to bring about the hoped-for respite: the Russians maintained their stranglehold on the division and the retreat soon degenerated into an ugly free-for-all without well-drawn battle lines. The Soviets were everywhere, creating islands of German resistance that had no option but to fight on alone in the hope of regaining contact later with the main group.

The Russian infantry had a new battlefield vehicle; armoured half-tracks for infantry transport supplied under the terms of the US Lend-Lease Pact. These machines were obviously very useful for getting Russian soldiers into and behind our lines, where they would disembark and immediately start fighting. The danger could be averted with anti-tank guns, but we had nothing more powerful than hand-grenades to do the job.

With a rumble of motor and a clanking of tread the half-tracks made for our positions. With no time to spare we discussed quickly how we were to combat this new peril, since hand-grenades seemed so unpromising a solution. Through field glasses I examined the approaching vehicles for a weak point. The front was armour plated with the driver located in a wheelhouse, vision being afforded by a viewing slit 30x10 centimetres in size. In my estimation the chance of a hit with a rifle shot was not good, but was probably the only way to stop the vehicle. I took careful note of the intervening terrain for likely course changes. The half-track was moving at walking pace. I loaded one explosive round and rolled a tent into a rest for the rifle barrel, aimed the weapon and watched the approach for my chance. Taking calm, measured breaths, I got the viewing slit in the crosswires and took up some pressure on the trigger. The machine was about 60 metres off when for a brief moment I saw the eyes of the driver through the viewing slit, possibly judging the ground ahead. I fired. A hit. At once the vehicle slewed and rutted sideways into a shell crater, the tracks continuing to turn and ensuring that it got well and truly stuck. The incumbent Russian soldiers abandoned the useless conveyance in panic and, being met at once by heavy fire from our riflemen, were forced back into the crater for protection. It appeared that the driver's cabin was partitioned off from the passenger area making it impossible to relieve him at the controls in an emergency. I had found the Achilles heel and hopes grew that this might be the answer. Using my last twenty explosive rounds I managed to kill or wound seven of the twelve half-track drivers that day. The other five got through our lines to unload their human freight, but the latter was not quality material and none lived to tell the tale. Although I had been successful, neighbouring divisions were breached at many points, forcing us to pull back yet again to an organized defensive line.

To our astonishment, OKH sent to our aid a number of Rumanian bomber aircraft and an anti-tank detachment. They destroyed twenty-four Russian tanks and gave us the breathing space needed to construct a new defensive line. After fighting for months without air support, the sight of friendly aircraft seemed almost surreal. Nevertheless, the regiment remained under severe pressure. Although the line held, we lost a third of our fighting personnel. Eventually the Soviets gave it up and switched their effort to a much weaker sector a few kilometres further on. A unit composed mainly of youngsters fresh from basic training was wiped out. In the uncanny silence the men of G.J.R. 144 grabbed a few hours' desperately needed sleep.

Chapter 6

Desperate Defence at Bakalov: Killing Horses, Cossacks, Women Snipers and Our Own

On 2 April 1944 Russian armour broke through the lines and encircled 3.G.D. There was no time to waste before attempting to escape. A very risky operation beckoned since we were equipped only with small arms and grenades, our only ally being the very inclement weather. That evening, in a blizzard reducing visibility to 50 metres, the thousand or so survivors of the regiment left their positions to form a long column two or three abreast. Everything possible was done to bring along the wounded; a fate worse than death awaited those who fell into the hands of the Russians. At the last farewell many of the wounded requested a pistol to determine for themselves the hour of their passing. A final handshake of mutual understanding – then the blizzard separated us from them for ever. While still in earshot we heard the first pistol shots ring out.

As usual I had my sniper's rifle wrapped in a tent and slung across my back, and carried an MP-40 at the breast for ready use. I was a member of the platoon protecting the right flank. We had been on the way for about an hour when I heard marching feet and snatches of conversation a few metres away to the right. I assumed that I had caught up with other platoon members in the poor visibility and fell back a little. Several minutes later a number of shadows became visible and I froze in horror as I heard the Russian in which they were conversing. We were marching parallel to a Soviet phalanx! I slipped away to rejoin our column and my expression was enough to convey the situation. Rapid hand signals passed from man to man. No word was spoken. Hardly daring to breathe, we bore away from the Russian unit. A short while later, but still enveloped in the darkness of early morning, the division came to a busy highway that crossed our direction of retreat. After an hour of watching the soldiery and traffic passing along it, the commander formed the opinion that we could not get the whole regiment across the highway without the procedure being seen, and the order was given to stage a surprise raid as a diversionary measure.

The assault platoon – five veterans and myself – lurked in the vegetation watching the passage of a supply column. Using a 40-metre gap between lorries, we sprang out a few metres in front of the oncoming vehicle and sprayed the driver's cab with a burst of MP-40 fire. Two of us lobbed grenades into the interior from the rear. The lorry sheered towards the undergrowth and as the grenades exploded, came to a rest at an angle straddling a ditch. The cab door opened, and in the pale light of the burning interior the driver stood for a brief moment, streaming blood and gurgling, before pitching face forward to the ground. At once we switched attention to the next lorry while the various companies of our regiment scurried across the highway. Within a few minutes the darkness had swallowed them up. We suffered no casualties.

After regrouping we continued our trudge towards the estuary of the Kutschurgan river. Our retreat ended 25 kilometres short of this natural defensive barrier near the town of Bakalov. Russian armour had already taken it and encircled five German divisions – 3.G.D. and 17., 258., 294. and 302. infantry divisions – in the process. The pocket was 8 kilometres long by 4 broad; Bakalov town was along the western perimeter, the highest topographical point being 140 metres. The German units were in a desperate plight, battalions being composed of half-strength companies armed only with light infantry weapons and grenades. The men were starving and in poor physical condition, but the fear of falling into Russian hands had concentrated their minds powerfully. Wittmann, commanding general 3.G.D. was in overall command, his immediate priority being to break out of the encirclement and reach the German lines along the west bank of the Kutschurgan. Besides the failure of logistics, the communications network had collapsed and messages were being passed by runners, wasting valuable hours that should have been devoted to planning the break-out strategy. The plan was finally settled upon during the afternoon of 5 April 1944, and at five o'clock 3.G.D. spearheaded the assault on Bakalov. The Russians were clearly surprised at the fighting spirit of these worn-down German troops and offered so little resistance that Bakalov was in our hands by nine that evening. G.J.R. 144 took over a small village a few kilometres west of the town.

This strategy had come into being following the receipt of information regarding a second encirclement nearby of which 24.*Armeekorps* was the victim. In order to kill two birds with one stone and give the break-out operation greater impact, General Wittmann decided that the two encirclements should be breached in concert, his main fear being that the *Armeekorps* movement would be too slow and stall. Unfortunately he could not contact 24.*Armeekorps*, so in order to bring his plan to fruition he took the dangerous step of suspending his own operation, capturing Bakalov and aiding the Armeekorps by having his own divisions bear the brunt of the Russian attack, G.J.R. 144 being among them.

The village, whose name I do not recall, was on the north-west perimeter of the encirclement, a typical rural hamlet of the region, twenty or so rude adobe dwellings with thatched roofs against a backdrop of scanty woodland. Together with ten riflemen I took possession of the ruins of an outlying farmhouse and prepared four hides with good cover and field of fire, special care being paid to rapid and protected movement between the five sites.

From about seven on the evening of 6 April the Russians began probing the perimeter at various places, and just before half nine the village dwellings were set alight as the prelude to a Cossack cavalry attack at a fast gallop. Highly mobile, they were quickly up to our positions, and in the flickering light of the fires it was almost impossible to get a clear shot at the riders. Accordingly, no matter how much we regretted it, we had to target the horses. I knew the neuralgic spots to aim for from my experiences sniping at Russian transport horses. If the bullet hit around the breastbone, the animal would collapse at once, often falling on the unseated rider. If hit in the kidney/intestinal region, the beast would rear up uncontrollably and eventually collapse, death following violent convulsions of the legs. I decided to aim for the breastbone if possible, and the midriff of those horses further away. The riflemen of my platoon would then pick off the Cossacks at leisure.

A number of charges ensued and within an hour the field was strewn with dead and dying horses and Cossacks. By then I was utterly sick of shooting horses. One Cossack got to within 50 metres of our position. I fired a round into the breastbone of his horse. The instant I did so, the animal jumped over a cadaver and the bullet ripped into the belly region, spilling out its intestines. The animal stopped, quivering; the rider seated as if paralysed on its back. The horse seemed to stare directly at me with wide, sad, questioning eyes, almost as if asking 'Why?' I gave the creature the *coup de grâce* in the forehead while a spray of MP-40 fire finished off the rider.

The next wave of cavalry made inroads into our positions, so close that I hid my sniper's rifle and fought with the MP-40. Our original eleven-man platoon had been whittled down to seven, holed up in the rubble of the farmhouse, in acute danger. There now followed a brief period of stupidity. The command centres of both sides, German and Russian, though possessed of only the sketchiest knowledge of the events in the village, opened fire with artillery and Stalin organs respectively. It lasted only a few minutes, wiped out a Cossack battalion, which was in the open and unprotected, and claimed a few *Jäger*. A short respite of eerie silence followed, and then came the next cavalry charge and death ride.

Our numbers, inadequate armaments and equipment, and few medical facilities dwindled under the pressure on our makeshift positions. The regiment, 300-strong at the beginning of the action, had 168 dead and wounded and was cut off from division. Its survival was now in doubt. In this precarious situation, regimental commander *Oberst* Lorch took upon himself the initiative of an immediate break-out attempt for early next morning. The companies were informed by despatch messengers. It meant leaving behind the worst of the wounded, but there was no alternative. The few surgeons and medics made the rounds classifying the wounded. Those listed to remain were given a pistol if they requested it. The arrangements were made swiftly and without sentimentality.

At midday the field reserve battalion north-west of Bakalov encountered extraordinarily accurate fire from a patch of dense woodland. Within a few minutes, eleven of their number had fallen to rifle bullets to the head or chest. The cry of 'Snipers!' drove the remainder to cover. Two company commanders who rose too high for a peep with binoculars paid with their lives, heads splayed by explosive rounds. The number of hits led to only one conclusion: the battalion was facing a sniper company! We had heard rumours of such a thing, but so far had only ever come up against marksmen operating singly. Lacking artillery or mortars the battalion was helpless. Fire was coming from the impenetrable vegetation of a small forest of conifers. Bursts of MG-fire had no apparent effect and the devastating response it evoked was usually fatal for the gunner who tried it. The *Jägers* fell back on protected positions such as behind the crumbling walls of a ruined collective. A despatch rider was sent to regimental HQ with a report and request for support. The battalion was hoping for a few heavy weapons to destroy the forest and those hiding in it, but nothing was available.

My reputation was known even to *Oberst* Lorch, but he probably considered it to be little more than a token response when he gave the messenger a written instruction for II./144 battalion command centre, ordering marksman Allerberger to engage a full Russian sniper company. Three hours later I was being briefed on the situation in the ruined collective.

The edge of the woods lay about 300 metres from these ruins. Given the depth of the wooded area I realized I would need to get nearer and tempt the Russians into shooting to betray their positions. This required a lure. I stuffed five grenade holders with grass and set a steel helmet on top of each. With a stick burnt to carbon I applied a nose, mouth and eyes. From my pack I brought out an umbrella frame minus the handle. I attached grasses and twigs to the spokes leaving just a small aperture free for vision. One hundred metres to the right of the building was a shallow depression skirted by bushes, an ideal spot for observation, which I could reach by crawling, unseen by the enemy. I agreed a handsignal at which one or other of the lures would be raised cautiously above the wall of the ruin. Twenty minutes later I was in position and set up my umbrella screen very carefully so that the movement, and the slight change to the scenery, were imperceptible.

I could now sweep the wood visually through binoculars. An analysis of the enemy rounds fired demonstrated that they had a good view of our positions. This suggested height, probably the treetops. It seemed unlikely to me, however, that expert snipers would make such a cardinal error and fire from a tree without adequate cover or an escape route.

I gave the agreed sign and the helmeted lures made a cautious show. A rain of bullets greeted them from the Russian lines. This provided me with a good view of several tree branches moving unnaturally under the pressure of the muzzle blast. The fact that the enemy was shooting from the treetops and that all five lures had attracted simultaneous fire, told me these were good marksmen lacking elementary fieldcraft. This lessened my worries somewhat as I contemplated taking on a very large handful of opponents.

I crawled back to the ruin at once and discussed the situation with the senior sergeant who was now commander of both companies following the death of the two officers. We set up five MGs in positions with a good arc of fire towards the woods and adequate local protection. To the side some distance away a rifleman waited to operate a lure. While I observed the woodland through binoculars, on my instruction he raised it from cover slowly. If it attracted a shot, I would identify the location from where it had originated. The MG would then fire a burst in the general direction of the trees, masking my aimed round. It was important to conceal from the Soviets the fact that they had a sniper working against them.

The tactical battle began. The lure rose and received three rounds as if to order. I saw the movement in the trees, took aim, waited for the MG to fire, then pulled the trigger. One by one the Russian snipers dropped from the trees, dead. After a quick change of position, a new round of the duel began. Within an hour I had reckoned on eighteen kills but still the lures drew fire. It was at about five in the afternoon, and an hour since the last shot had been loosed off from the woods, that the sergeant decided on storming the woods under the cover of the two MGs and myself. They reached the woods unopposed, looked with astonishment at the corpses and gesticulated wildly for us to join them. Cautiously, unhappy with the deceptive lull, we crossed the open land to the trees.

A young woman, scarcely twenty, lay on her stomach, her rifle below her. A *Jäger* turned the inert body to one side to retrieve her weapon. Her right hand was inside her uniform jacket, covering the gaping wound in her chest. As the *Jäger* bent down she drew a Tokarev pistol and, gurgling blood, mouthed the expression 'Death to the fascists' before pulling the trigger with the last ounce of her strength. As the German soldier dived to one side, the bullet grazed the seat of his pants. As he rolled free, his MP-40 came free and he fired into the female torso, ending her valiant career.

It was the first time we had come up against female front-line warriors. As we stood over their dead bodies, some with shattered, bloody masks of flesh and bone instead of faces and features, we all felt a sense of revulsion and shame even though we knew that there had been no alternative. If we had known in advance that we were facing women, the knowledge might well have interfered with our determination to rout out the opposition, and resulted in many more casualties amongst our ranks.

The use of sniper-groups was a Russian tactic that originated under German influence. During the post-First World War phase of mutual cooperation, the Weimar Republic had supplied the Soviets with the technology to manufacture telescopic sights, the use of such optics being unknown hitherto among the Russian forces. While the *Wehrmacht* was still issuing old *Reichswehr* sights in 1940, the Red Army had developed a comprehensive Sniper Branch with modern weapons. There were single operators, sniper and observer pairs, sniper pairs and companies up to sixty strong. From the beginning of the German invasion, Russian snipers harried the *Wehrmacht*, inflicting serious losses, particularly on officers, and by this means were often able to halt for days the advance of infantry lacking heavy weapons. In the heady period of victories in 1941, OKH dismissed the sniper danger as an irrelevance, and only in 1942 was the problem grudgingly acknowledged. The lack of a useful sniper-rifle for the *Wehrmacht* was now critical, and the Modell 41 with 1.5x magnification issued as a target aid for precision shooting with the 98k carbine over long distances was found totally unsuitable. There was nothing for it but to improvise while German industry tackled the whole problem. The simple solution was to use captured Russian weapons. Guidelines for snipers were issued for the first time towards the end of 1942 but the first firm instructions in rifle use and sniper deployment were not available until May 1943. According to these rules, snipers were to be directly under the control of company commanders and exempt from daily routine. Their role was special reconnaissance and sharpshooting. As their survival depended to a large degree on their remaining unseen by the enemy, the veterans among them developed a knack for wandering terrain unnoticed. Contrary to the later official training manuals or propaganda films, full dress camouflage was rarely used. It was time-consuming, required a lot of material and restricted freedom of movement. Every sniper who lived long enough to adjust to the life used improvised camouflage aids that could be donned or erected quickly, interfered little with movement and were easy to transport. For myself I preferred an umbrella frame with the crooked handle cut off. It was easy to dress with grasses and twigs to blend in with the natural environment and big enough to screen me. When not in use it was easily collapsible and fitted into my battle pack.

At first light on 6 April 1944, *Gruppe* Lorch attacked the encirclement at the northern perimeter below the 140-metre spot height, all reserves being called upon in the desperate struggle to escape. The official records speak of an heroic action planned and executed to the last detail, but the reality was organized chaos blessed with good fortune. Many men lost their nerve and fled in panic beforehand. Shortly before the decisive attack I was queuing at the last field kitchen to fill my tea-flask when through the swathes of morning mist there came the sound of roaring motors and squeaking tracks. Everybody stared towards the noise, straining to make out the tanks. There was still nothing to see when an hysterical voice yelled, 'It's Ivan! He's here! Tanks!' Most of the *Jäger* broke and ran. The catering sergeant mounted his horse in a flying leap and whipped the animal into a gallop, tea from the open containers aboard the wheeled field kitchen slopping in all directions. A few of the veterans tried to halt the panic. A few cuffs to the ear and kicks to the rear brought some of the men to their senses, but more than half had disappeared into the mist behind the field kitchen. The remainder waited for the death-dealing T-34s to materialize through the fog, and a few minutes later the German SP-guns, which had been sent up unannounced in support of the break-out, made their appearance. It was another half hour before the last of the fleeing made their sheepish return, and accepted a kick in the pants as a disciplinary measure for their action.

By evening the break-out by *Gruppe* Lorch through the Russian lines had been achieved. The main force, *Gruppe* Wittmann, forced the Russian encirclement north-west of Bakalov and German units poured through in disorder. The objective was the Kutschurgan river via the town of Getmanzy. It was several hours before fighting units and engineers re-established contact between the respective groups. We had progressed about seven miles westward from the perimeter and had reached the railway tunnel south of the town of Petrovsky when there occurred a most dreadful incident amongst our own troops.

My own battalion had been reduced to a pitiful rump of about sixty men. As always in these retreats, and common to both sides, 'scorched earth' policy meant leaving the enemy with an infrastructure in smouldering ruins. Orders had been received to blow up the railway tunnel south of Petrovsky, which for the time being was an important conduit for our troops. Our battalion was the last through it, and we saw the sappers making their last preparations to dynamite it. *Hauptmann* Kloss told the engineer's officer that a troop of our own engineers was following as a rearguard and that the demolition should be delayed until they were safely through the tunnel, but the explosives-sappers were jittery, and when the rearguard had not shown within ten minutes, they dynamited the tunnel. Another ten minutes had passed when two filthy dirty and distraught battalion engineers of the rearguard rejoined *Gruppe* Lorch and reported that the tunnel had been blown up as they were passing through it. The two men had only survived because they had gone ahead as the advance party of the rearguard. The story was received with incredulity, then anger and rage. The battalion marched on and half an hour later reached the agreed assembly point. A sentry called out suddenly: 'Stop! Stand still! Password!'

A rifleman of the advance party told him where to stuff his password and kept walking. The following column watched with horror as a machine-gunner opened fire, raking the back of the infantryman. Seconds later all threw themselves prostrate to the ground. Our commander pushed his way through to the front and shouted, 'Cease fire, you arsehole. This is the Kloss battalion. Fetch your superior officer immediately.' A few minutes later an *Oberleutnant* appeared and asked a few questions, which Kloss answered in bad humour. Finally he received the instruction to approach alone. Kloss rose cautiously and, holding his pistol at the ready, went forward. He was trembling with rage. At the feet of the *Oberleutnant*, Kloss saw the killer-gunner sitting behind his weapon. He was no more than a youngster, convulsed with fear. Kloss roared at him: 'You filthy shit, you have killed a comrade, and now I am going to kill you, you swine!' His hysteria built to a high pitch and became rapidly uncontrollable before he gave a long cry and emptied the magazine of his pistol into the youth, who watched his death at the hands of a German officer with eyes wide in panic. The nearest riflemen wrestled Kloss to the ground, slapped his face and forced him to calm himself. Aside from these men and the *Oberleutnant*, the latter of whom understood this momentary nervous breakdown on Kloss' part, there were no witnesses to the incident, and thus no further action was ever taken. The two soldiers had merely 'Fallen for the Führer and Greater Germany', but as to the circumstances of their passing, nobody could be found subsequently who knew.

That evening *Gruppe* Lorch re-established radio contact with a neighbouring Wittmann battalion to the south of us. The outlook was not good: the structure of the latter had disintegrated and numerous independent units were involved in continual skirmishing during the 25-kilometre chase to the Kutschurgan river. Towards ten, Wittmann's HQ picked up a signal from 97 Jg.Div. calling all German units behind a new front line on the bank of the river, 97 Jg.Div. having prepared crossing points protected with the support of 257 Inf.Div. It was fairly desperate, for the Russians in hot pursuit were lobbing large quantities of mortars into the retreating columns. Wittmann assembled his last artillery pieces into a battery and surprised them with a bombardment. It gained his advanced companies a breathing space, but the Russians were prompt to turn their attentions to the breach in the encirclement through which *Gruppe* Wittmann was still pouring. The enemy opened up a withering fire but this was countered by desperate hand-to-hand fighting supported by sniper fire concentrated on Russian MG positions and mortars. After an hour the determination of the Soviets wilted and the breach held. It was a moonless night and little further contact was reported.

At nine on the morning of 7 April 1944 the first of *Gruppe* Wittmann's force crossed the Kutschurgan. His five divisions totalled 4,500 men: 3.G.D. had less than a thousand survivors. We kept on going for three more days, crossing the Dniester on 10 April. It was a portentous moment, the end of Barbarossa, for we had passed beyond the territorial limits of the Soviet Union and entered Rumanian Bessarabia. After three years of the most bitter fighting and horrendous losses, all now knew beyond the slightest doubt that the war was being brought ever closer to the Reich. The enemy we faced on this front had to be held, for ever if possible. A tiny spark of hope still glimmered that somewhere, somehow, we could stop him permanently.

Whenever I had time I would reflect on what made a good sniper. In warfare, soldiers are faced with the constant threat of serious injury, mutilation and death. Many crumble under the psychological burden and panic under pressure. This often manifests in firing off wildly or creating a mental disposition to run once things begin to deteriorate. A soldier's resistance to stress determines his quality far more than his marksmanship or other technical ability. For this reason, a sniper in prospect is difficult to spot away from the front. In particular, the selection and training of a future sniper based only on shooting ability is a grave error, for the soldier must be possessed of a high degree of self-control and have nerves of steel. Good accurate shooting can be learnt, and the value placed on it by the military in the initial stages of the selection process is exaggerated. The maximum effective range for a rifle under battle conditions is 400 metres, but as a general rule half that when aiming to hit the greatest surface area of the target centrally. Absolute reliability, adherence to military routine, ruthlessness and the art of sharpshooting make the sniper, not target-shooting at 100 metres.

So far as I can recall, the only occasion when I dressed in full camouflage gear occurred shortly after our arrival at the Dniester. We set about making our trenches homely and created a sort of village organization based on the regiment. From thin air all kinds of utensils were produced, wash-rooms and showers, barbers' saloons. Poultry appeared as if by magic, treasured for their flesh and eggs and naturally guarded by their owners like the crown jewels. Foxes – the human kind – lurked in the shadows, casting covetous eyes at what was on offer, and the successful poultry thief was a man to be revered among the lower orders.

The battalion despatch runners, to whom I was on semi-permanent detachment, had little opportunity to cultivate company life. Their efforts for a better diet had led them down the slippery road to crime. Their distrustful comrades watched them like hawks. But it was only a question of time before The Big Coup. Freely wandering the battalion lines it had come to my notice that the CSM of the neighbouring company owned a hen, named Josephine, which could be relied upon to produce an egg daily for the CSM's table or barter. A single bird was an ideal target for abduction, for if one exercised due caution the danger of a general cacophony, such as one might expect from a disturbed flock, was absent. I was elected unanimously for the job on account of my fieldcraft, since my 'Red Indian instincts', not to mention 'catlike agility', made me 'the perfect choice'.

It was a night of the new moon and fully overcast, ideal for a commando raid of this kind. While the others stoked the fire and prepared the cooking utensils, for the first and only time I put on full camouflage dress, blacked my hands and face, and attached leafy vegetation to my peaked cap and uniform until I looked like a bush. After receiving brief instruction from a former poultry farmer in the technique of killing a bird by hand, I disappeared into the darkness, rustling lightly in the wind. Like a fox I slunk into the HQ of the neighbouring company. The hen was sleeping in her nest, a lovingly furbished wicker basket for artillery ammunition. There was a sentry about 20 metres away in conversation with a friend: they were sharing a cigarette and every time either took a drag they raised a steel helmet to their faces so that the glow from the cigarette should not betray them to the enemy. I was more on tenterhooks than normal for this was looting and the penalty for detection could easily be the firing squad. Scarcely daring to breathe, I lifted the catch of the wicker basket. The hen was sleeping with her head under a wing. I could not afford to make a mistake. Keeping the lid up by resting it against my forehead, I seized the bird with both hands and swiftly put her to sleep – permanently. With a glance at the sentry, who was chatting and had seen nothing, I stuffed the dead Josephine inside my camouflage jacket and disappeared as silently as I had arrived. Within fifteen minutes the bird was plucked and eviscerated, and the inedible evidence carefully buried.

On the morning following the grand feast, the CSM appeared and declared that he was in no doubt as to the perpetrators of the crime. 'Which filthy swine stole my hen, it can only have been your company because the thief's footprints lead here. None of my men would have dared lay a hand on Josephine, I would have shot him personally.' Our facial expressions of hurt and reproach at the implication appeared to weaken his resolve and, muttering to himself, the CSM withdrew after making it clear that he had narrowed his suspicions down to one person, but had no proof. He promised not to relent, however, and should the evidence he needed be unearthed in due course, the person involved would be court-martialled and shot for looting.

Chapter 7

Balmy Days on
the Dniester

3.G.D., desperately short of men and weapons, received a token influx, mainly survivors from other divisions, which helped little. We were also given a stiffening of Rumanian units. Our Axis ally was very poorly equipped and armed, lacked battle experience and proved of equally limited value. On 17 April 1944, only ten days after our arrival on the Dniester, orders came for a third of 3.G.D. to bolster another sector of the front under serious threat. It was my good fortune to remain behind on this occasion, for G.J.R. 138 '*Kampfgruppe* Rohde' was to suffer fearful casualties with over 800 dead.

For a few weeks I enjoyed halcyon days with the remainder of the division. May was a warm, gentle month, and after the troubles we had gone through to get here, our front line with a river view on the banks of the Dniester came as a delightful surprise.

Germans and Russians faced each other across the river within the range of heavy infantry weapons, but limited their hostilities to the occasional exchange of mortar and MG-fire and the odd commando raid to break the monotony. The river was about 400 metres wide and did not allow for reconnaissance outings by snipers. I visited the battalion trenches daily but did no more than fire the occasional precision shot at targets spotted by our infantry. Aiming at a Soviet head 400 metres off had a 30 per cent chance of a hit, but the effect on morale of 70 per cent hair's breadth misses from a sniper's rifle made the effort worthwhile.

As regular as clockwork I made my calls on the trenches. The Russians had been lying low for days, for they were loath to show themselves once they had received notice that an expert sniper was present in the German lines opposite. That particular morning I had been with the MG-gunners surveying the enemy positions without finding a worthwhile target, and decided to pass the afternoon at the northern end of the battalion's trenches. I rarely went there, for they overlooked a bend in the river a kilometre wide, and I considered them valueless. Sometimes the belligerents exchanged MG bursts, but the range was far too long for a rifle.

In our positions the mood was rather like a holiday camp. The May heat wave had gone on and on, and we had become accustomed to stripping to the waist to soak up the sunshine. Improvised showers had been rigged using the waters of the Dniester and wonderful small picnics of ship's biscuit, tinned marmalade and ersatz coffee were quite common. At the northernmost trench I was invited to partake, the fare being all the more delicious for having been 'liberated' from the *Kübelwagen* of two artillery officers who had visited the area the day before on a reconnaissance outing. During the conversation, an MG-gunner mentioned hearing unusual sounds borne on the wind from the Russian side of the river. He thought the nearest thing to it he had ever heard was at a municipal outdoor swimming pool on a bank holiday weekend. This awakened my interest, and I decided to investigate. Between this last trench and the southernmost of the neighbouring battalion was a stretch of unoccupied terrain which promised a different view of the Russian lines. About 1,500 metres further on was a small hill covered with dense bushy undergrowth offering extensive cover for observation purposes. I climbed to the hilltop from behind and peered cautiously through the high grass between two bushes. Through my binoculars I saw an extraordinary scene. Hidden from the view of our positions was a small bay. The Soviets obviously believed themselves so safe there that it was being used as a holiday beach and, so far as I could make out, sentries and lookouts had been dispensed with. I estimated the range as 600 metres. The day was windless and the air dry. I decided to try a body shot at one of the bathers over this enormous distance. Why did I do this? It was a mixture of several things: displeasure at our unspeakable opponents doing anything that remotely approached having a good time; my personal ambition to score a kill at this distance; and my belief in the need to make our determination unmistakably clear to the Russians at every opportunity that we were as serious as they were.

I selected the largest and most immobile target. On the slope of the river bank opposite, a group of Russians lay sunbathing in the sand, their bodies facing towards me. As I was in an elevated shooting position, it was almost the same as if they were standing. With my bayonet I dug out some clumps of earth and moulded them into a firm rest for the barrel of my rifle. I lined the crosswires of the telescopic sight above the head of the selected victim, breathed regularly and calmly a few times, took up pressure on the trigger, held my breath, concentrated on the target one last time, and fired. Like the crack of a whip the projectile broke the stillness. After the recoil I had the target under observation within a fraction of a second; the bullet entered the Russian just above the navel, and he folded like a penknife. I even heard his cry of pain and the panic-filled voices of his comrades. As he rolled to one side I saw the giant pool of blood he left in the sand. The other Russians had scampered for cover and left him to it. After a few minutes his movements froze and death took him.

Meanwhile I saw through my binoculars a number of uniformed Russians appear above the slope. It looked like they meant business. A few moments later I heard the dull retort of a mortar being fired, the grenade landed on the river bank below me and exploded. Obviously they had spotted my position and I had to beat a hasty retreat. Weasel-like, I sneaked away and ran down the back of the hill to our trenches. As I did so their mortars got the range of my abandoned hiding place and shredded the hilltop.

Upon my return, the host of the coffee hour received me with a certain hostility. 'Shit, did you have to?' he demanded and, turning to his men, told them to get their bunks ready 'since Ivan is soon going to give us hell', adding darkly, 'Herr Fancy Shooter here simply couldn't resist spoiling our idyll.' Hardly had the words fallen from his lips than the first MG bursts whistled over our heads, followed by a brief mortar bombardment which fortunately fell long and caused no damage. During the general hiatus I made myself scarce, since I had no wish to expose myself to any further abuse. The next day the occasional precision shot hit our positions. Nobody was hurt but it told us that the Russians had called up a specialist to settle my hash. He would be disappointed, however, for a cross-river duel was out of the question. All the same, I was doubly cautious and watchful.

Around 25 May 1944 our period of tranquillity ended. The remnant of G.J.R. 138 returned and 3.G.D. was ordered to the Aurel Pass in the Carpathian mountains. Our new positions followed the course of the Moldau river separating the two warring armies. In addition to the watery barrier, the wooded slopes of the gently rising mountains provided us with good cover while the land on the Russian-held side was open plain and easily observed. For once the fates had smiled kindly on the division, for the Russian strongpoint was well to the north of its positions and locally the Soviets were interested in nothing more alarming than the occasional skirmish.

Another unexpected period of tranquillity thus became our lot. Really fine summer weather offered our exhausted troops a chance of modest rest and recuperation. We re-adjusted quickly to trench life, and slept in earth bunkers entered through a low porch of corrugated iron sheeting. A trestle table and benches for eight under the trees endowed the place with a holiday camp look again.

For the man in the field, the tension of constant warring very often resulted in a voracious sexual appetite. The outlet for this natural desire for sex was only available when a unit found itself in a relatively quiet situation. While officers and senior NCOs would consort with market girls, female volunteers and *Wehrmacht* auxiliaries, the common foot soldier was rarely accommodated because of his low rank or standing. The German Army considered rape a very serious matter and the penalty was severe. Local brothels, if they existed at all, would be unable to cope with the demand when a whole division arrived, and in any case, OKH opposed such establishments on principle as sources of venereal disease. Many men actively sought infection with gonorrhoea as a means to lose their 'fit for the front' category. (The other main venereal scourge of the time, syphilis, was barely treatable and a condom gave no protection. After contagion there would be a period of remission of several, perhaps many years before its effects began to show, and it was therefore worthless to the malingerer. Gonorrhoea showed after a few days, was highly contagious, did not go away and required immediate treatment.) In order to provide a sexual service and guard against its disadvantages, it was the practice along secure sectors of the front to allow a *Wehrmacht* field brothel to be set up. For the purpose of preventing the infection and spread of gonorrhoea, these brothels had more medics in attendance than girls. Preventive treatment for everybody followed a sex session and was painful and extremely unpleasant, involving as it did a large syringe being forced into the urethra for the purpose of releasing 100 millilitres of a green sulphanomide solution into the genital tubes. All handling of the body parts was carried out by the medic. The disinfectant had to be retained for five minutes and could then be urinated free. It was reported that the latter sensation of relief was more orgasmic than the session which preceded it.

Where an advanced stage of gonorrhoea was diagnosed, the sufferer was sent to one of several special hospitals known collectively as '*Ritterburg*' where the purpose was not only to cure the disease, but to deter the patient from unhealthy future contacts by an unnecessarily barbarous method of treatment and care. Those who became reinfected were court-martialled on a charge of self-mutilation.

A *Wehrmacht* brothel had arrived in the local town. It was staffed by five Rumanian girls who charged five Reichsmarks. Privacy was afforded by a *Wehrmacht* blanket draped over the doorway, behind which lurked a sadistic medic waiting for the *Jäger*'s session of pleasure to terminate, and his own to begin. I had recently met up again with sniper Josef Roth, and in our long conversations the brothel question would occasionally arise. Neither of us had known sexual contact with a woman in our lives and we agreed that this might be the last chance for the experience before death. We were still arguing the pros and cons when I noticed a supply sergeant who had delivered some ammunition and was now sitting on the running board of an Opel Blitz lorry waiting for orders. By his red beard I recognized him as the Viking who had been my platoon commander during my first five days at the front. He had divined our intentions and made us listen to an account of his own experiences at the same brothel, stationed elsewhere, a few weeks earlier. His description of the drastic preventive treatment left us both in no doubt that the brief few minutes of pleasure were not worth the consequences. Being of good Catholic upbringing I was in any case not 100 per cent certain that I wanted my first sexual experience to take place in a *Wehrmacht* brothel, and by the end of the war had resisted all further temptations.

By some miracle the division had been returned unexpectedly to its full quota in men and materials. The officers probably knew by now that we were at full strength for the last time: they had seen the writing on the wall long previously. What kept them all going was the determination to hold off the Russians for as long as possible.

The Soviets were massing for another onslaught against the few German and Rumanian divisions. The calm before the storm would be the last opportunity for the few long-servers in the division who had more or less come through everything without serious injury to see their families, perhaps for one last time. So far as possible they were granted leave. At age nineteen and having served ten months on

5. *Generalfeldmarschall* Ferdinand Schörner. A man of considerable personal valour, he was noted as a ruthless disciplinarian, although this may have been because he was always placed in the most difficult situations where his loyalty to the Nazi cause ensured that he obeyed his orders to the letter.

...ajor Kloss, commander G.J.R. ...4./3.G.D., fell 10 November 1944.

7. General Paul Klatt, commander 3.G.D.

8. Difficult terrain in eastern Czechoslovakia for Schörner's final resistance to the Soviets.

9. Poorly equipped German mountain troops pass through a rail marshalling yard during the long retreat.

active front line duty in the German Army I amounted to a veteran, but had a lower priority for leave than fathers of children and men with two years in the Army. Moreover, snipers could not be spared from the front. Theoretically my chances of leave were nil until *Hauptmann* Kloss, my battalion commander, who held me in regard, found a way to resolve my difficulty.

In the last few months of 1943 at the larger military depots, firing ranges were introduced for sniper training. The course lasted four weeks. Those taking part were recruited from recent conscripts but also included veterans from the front who had been identified by their company commanders as good prospects. They would receive a sniper rifle with telescopic sight and instruction in the art. In Austria, *Gebirgsjäger* sniper training was held at the Seetaleralpe military depot near Judenburg. This was not too far from my home village. *Hauptmann* Kloss had down-graded me to a 'sniper prospect' in need of honing to a fine edge and thus suitable for training at Seetaleralpe. Since I was almost at home there anyway, ten days leave had been added, to be taken at the end of the course.

A few hours before my departure on 30 May 1944, I handed my Russian rifle and telescopic sight to the regimental armourer. In my hearing he passed it to another young *Jäger* saying, 'You see all the little notches carved in the stock and hand-guard? Each is one less Russian. To receive this weapon is honour and duty. Do your best and show Sepp on his return that you have been worthy of it.'

Hearing these heroic words the young rifleman looked rather embarrassed and I laid my hand on his shoulder saying: 'Don't go mad, just remain on the alert and keep your head out of sight making the rounds.' From a breast pocket I produced a handful of bullets carefully wrapped in a handkerchief, my little stock reserved for special cases and, pressing them into his hand, said: 'I probably won't be needing these any more. They are explosive rounds, so go easy with them, the supply is limited to what we can steal from the Russians. Keep on the armourer's good side, and he will keep his eye open for captured ammunition and put it to one side for you. Tell me in six weeks how you got on.'

The engine of the Opel Blitz lorry roared up impatiently and I hoisted myself over the tailboard, the last of eleven leave-takers to board. When I shook the hand of my replacement in parting, an indefinable presentiment of his death made me shiver. The thought came to me suddenly: 'Poor devil, he isn't long for this world.'

'Are you ladies through with your fond farewells yet?' the driver bawled from his cab and, without waiting for an answer, stepped on the gas pedal. Our comrades disappeared behind a thick cloud of dust and exhaust fumes. A feeling of light-heartedness swept over me at my temporary release from the war, but it was tempered by bad conscience at leaving my friends in the lurch. The past year had blotted out my former existence, and the daily struggle to survive had become my only reality.

Chapter 8

Respite: Sniper Training at Judenburg, Summer 1944

It took a few days to realize for sure that the war had turned its back on me. The peaceful landscapes through which the train puffed its way on the five-day run to Judenburg seemed like an anachronism. When I alighted at the station, a driver on an errand gave me a lift to the depot in his *Kübelwagen*. I viewed the course with mixed feelings, for my recollections of basic training, with its endless shouting and purposeless drill, were not my fondest memories of the German Army. I had only agreed to accept the course because it offered a couple of weeks of proper nutrition, regular sleep and the chance of a few days' leave with my family. Therefore I was all the more surprised to receive an almost cordial welcome from the CSM in his office. No standing stiffly to attention, no heel-clicking, just a friendly introductory talk about the course and accommodation. It was clear that this was an advanced course for specialists and not the brutal indoctrination of course material by rote.

The Army depot occupied a large area of terrain. The sniper school nestled in a remote barrack complex. I shared a hut with four eighteen-year-olds from Mittenwald who were fresh from basic training at Kufstein and had been sent from there directly to sniper school, having impressed instructors with their stoical calm and outstanding faculty of observation. My glance fell at once upon a text in gothic lettering nailed to a wall:

1. The sniper is the hunter among soldiers!
2. His job is difficult and demands the dedication of body, soul and mind.
3. Only a thoroughly convinced and steadfast soldier can become a sniper.

4. It is only possible to destroy an enemy if one has learnt to hate and persecute him with all the strength in one's soul!
5. A sniper is a man set apart from the common soldier.
6. He fights unseen.
7. His strength is based on Red Indian-like use of territory linked to perfect camouflage, catlike agility and masterly use of his rifle.
8. Awareness of his abilities gives him the sureness and superiority which guarantee success.

These heroic words did not leave me unimpressed and I felt a certain pride rise within me, yet at the same time I remembered the reality of war and its merciless nature. As you die, I thought, all these fine words mean nothing.

Next day, Monday 5 June 1944, the course entitled *Scharfschützen Ausbildung Kompanie WK XVIII* began with instruction on rifles with telescopic sights. Our instructor was a sergeant minus a leg, and nearly all the staff were experienced campaigners with partial invalidity. Many were former snipers who had worked out the fieldcraft for themselves at the front until their wounds deprived them of their 'fit for the front' category. The course had sixty trainees, divided into twelve groups of five each, each group having its own instructor to guarantee the almost personal transmission of knowledge.

A table top was laid with four rifles, three Mauser K98k and a weapon new to us, each fitted with an optical sight. At the front I had heard rumours of a new semi-automatic, but had never seen one. This was the Walther self-loading Modell 43 with a Voigtländer Modell 4 sight. The Mausers were fitted respectively with the 15cm long Modell 41, the 6-power Zeiss Zielsechs and the Hensoldt Modell Dialytan.

After an explanation from the tutors regarding the efficiency of the four optics and mountings, they spoke about the Mauser carbine with Hensoldt sight specifically, this being considered the best and firmest combination, and the rifle with which each of us would be issued. In the afternoon we range-tested each of the four rifles. I was amazed at the wide field of vision, the brilliance of the Zeiss and Hensoldt optics, which were far superior to my Russian scope. On the other hand, the latter and the Voigtlander were virtually similar, and although the Walther self-loading rifle was a pleasant weapon to fire, since part of the recoil force was absorbed by the automatic reload mechanism, its accuracy fell short of the Mauser carbine. For amusement we fired the semi-automatic fitted with the ZF 41 sight, and agreed with the tutors that its designers must have made it as a practical joke.

After these free exercises we returned to ordinary rifle shooting with the conventional K98k carbine over open sights from 50 to 300 metres: free standing, kneeling, lying. Ammunition was freely available and the usual safety drills were dispensed with to allow us to keep up the momentum.

Next morning found us in the countryside for distance estimation exercises and the tactical assessment of terrain, the afternoon we spent shooting, and in fact there was almost no day in which shooting was absent from the timetable. During the week we were taught trench digging and camouflage. I learnt nothing new and went through the motions. Some of the camouflage ideas were very costly in time and materials, and of questionable value in practice. Hollowed-out tree trunks, a full body camouflage of tree bark, a fake milestone of wood to hide a slit trench: these were ideas that seemed to have no practical value. In my experience, camouflage needed to be quickly prepared, effective and improvised from the simplest materials available, limiting the sniper as little as possible in movement.

On the last day of the first week, we were introduced to 'The Shooting Garden'. About fifty metres from the firing stands was a miniature landscape designed to resemble a valley with roads and a village reduced to scale. Three small-calibre Army sports rifles were provided: the Walther Deutsches Sport Modell with 4 power Oigee sight, the Menz Deutscher Sport and the Gustloff Wehrsportgewehr, the latter two both fitted with the ZF 41 optic.

The exercise was to keep the landscape under observation and shoot at small papier mâché figures as soon as they appeared at windows, between houses or behind trees. Tiny cars and horse-drawn carts moving across the landscape were also to be brought under fire as the situation demanded. In this exercise my practical experience came to the fore. My trained eye picked out the slightest movement and it was rarely more than thirty seconds before my shot hit the target. I used only the Oigee sight – the ZF 41 had an optic of small diameter and such a poor field of fire that all trainees without exception rejected it as useless for sniper work. I obtained a perfect score in the exercise. The course tutors knew that I had some sniper experience, but did not know the extent. A perfect score was so rare that they already suspected there was little more they could teach me.

The shooting garden received frequent visits from us throughout the course. The arrangement of scenery and location of targets was changed regularly. To encourage competition between the candidates, our daily scores were recorded and the eventual winner received the reward of a certificate and a large sack of groceries. We were required to keep a small personal notebook to list our scores and jot down observations on the terrain. On the battlefield it was supposed to serve to note our witnessed kills as well. My room-mates advised me to always use code and omit my name as owner, and most important of all to lodge my claimed kills on an anonymous sheet with the CSM, the purpose being to avoid my being identified as a sniper if captured. Any German soldier who fell into Russian hands and was identified as a sniper could expect to be tortured to death. I saw some of the younger trainees blanch when they were told this.

Monday of the second week was a red-letter day. That morning a lorry arrived from Mauser, and we helped unload a number of crates stencilled 'byf'. They contained brand-new K98k carbines fitted with the 4-power Hensoldt sight on an adjustable mounting. Each man received a personal issue, its registration number being entered into our individual course books. It would become our personal property upon passing the course successfully. The younger soldiers without battlefield experience were very keen to qualify for this very reason. On inspection I found the weapon to be quite a lot shorter than the Russian rifle I had been using, but the optic was far better. I could hardly wait to test the weapon that afternoon, and after the first few rounds I concluded that this was the sniper weapon which led the field.

Our first issue of sniper ammunition was distributed from boxes bearing the designation '*Anschuss*' to distinguish them from ordinary rounds. The instructor explained that the projectiles had been prepared individually to ensure maximum precision. When at the front, we were to ask our armourers for them specifically. We calibrated the optical sight over a distance of 100 metres. This was done by removing the breech and placing the carbine on sandbags on the range table for stability. When the centre of the target was lined up through the barrel, the rifleman coincided the optic by adjusting two screws on the rear foot of the mounting using a special key. After this rough calibration, fine adjustment followed during practical shooting.

The day ended with instructions never to allow the weapon out of one's hands and throughout the remainder of the course the trainees always carried the weapon with them. All rooms had a rifle keep for use at night. The idea was to instil in us the need to protect the optic, for any hard jolt could spoil the calibration. I had learnt this the hard way during my first few days as a sniper at the front and it now came as second nature, but the other trainees had difficulty handling the carbine with kid gloves. Since the calibration procedure had to be repeated if the weapon was knocked or dropped, the culprit was punished with twenty push-ups and thirty knee-bends holding the rifle above his head.

The following day we were shown a film entitled *Choice of, and Constructing Positions*. We were astonished to find that it was in Russian with German subtitles and had been recorded in 1935. It gave an impressive insight into the high standard of Russian training. The instructor told us how difficult Russian snipers had made the advance of German forces in 1941/2. Compared to them, we had known nothing. Our losses among command staff from snipers had been devastating. If a unit lacked heavy infantry weapons, a Russian sniper company could pin it down all day. We had tried to get back on level terms using captured optics. On a personal note he remarked that on his last day at the front he had personally escaped death by a whisker. Tilting his head a little to one side to enable us all to see the scar tissue on the left side of his face from which his glass eye stared, he explained that a sniper's bullet had struck his Zeiss binoculars and saved his life. 'Ivan has professionals, make no mistake about it,' he warned, 'and if you notice that your opposite number is gunning for you, clear out, and never fire a second shot from the same position.'

The film held nothing new for me and I had begun to doze in the darkness, eyes half open, when a scene aroused my interest. It showed a Russian sniper company climbing to the treetops at the edge of a wood. The subtitles read: 'Treetops with plenty of leaf are an outstanding position! The rifleman cannot be seen, but has a good view of the landscape and an outstanding field of fire!'

These film sessions were informal and we were at liberty to interject at any time. The instructor would then stop the projector to allow a point to be made. Indicating that I wanted to speak, the film was stopped, and I recounted my tale about the female sniper company at Bakalov. After I had finished speaking, the instructor broke the silence and said, 'Listen closely, *Junge*, the *Jäger* knows what he is talking about, he has already spent a year at the front. Get it into your heads that you make a mistake only once, and in 90 per cent of cases you have shit your last. So, note well everything you hear on this course, that something may well save your arse in the field.'

To be on the course, eating and sleeping regularly, and not in constant fear for my life, was a delight. My thoughts often strayed to 3.G.D., but the censored newspaper reports gave no clear picture. Occasionally the instructors passed on information gleaned from leave-takers, and from this it appeared that the sector was quiet and the line had held.

Field theory was put into practice over the next few days to test the independence of the individual. We were lodged in a common shelter and had to select a suitable spot to dig a personal slit trench for occupation early next morning. The battle scenario was that two enemy snipers had 'No-Man's-Land' pinned down: any observed movement of the trainee meant his end, the purpose being to teach him to lie low and consider personal strategy for the next day. Near each 'sniper' was a tutor who refereed on claimed 'kills'. The trainees were therefore confined to their individual trenches until night fell. Horror showed itself on almost every face. The value of the exercise was obvious to me, of course. To remain more or less immobile in one spot from five in the morning to eleven at night brought with it questions about food, water and the natural functions. As a veteran, I chose and prepared a position that took all this into account. My comrades preferred for the most part to cover their helmets with a light camouflage of grass and fresh twigs.

The day of the ordeal was baking hot. By noon the trainees were bathed in sweat, their limbs ached and bodily functions needed to be exercised and could not be. Early on I had got a look at the terrain and spotted where the instructors were positioned. From then on it was a piece of cake. I had prepared my slit trench sufficiently deep that I could lay well below the surface. In the field this provided not only good protection against shell splinters but enabled me to spend long periods of inactivity in relative comfort. A small drainage hole for urinating was reached by a turn to one side. I had trained my body to evacuate early morning and the problem of solid waste did not arise. As a veteran at the front it was routine to carry a small supply of water and dry tack. At Seetaleralpe I simply made myself comfortable and spent the day sleeping and chewing biscuit and black bread. When darkness fell and the order came to return to barracks, I found many of my comrades at their last gasp. Most had wet their trousers and worse, attracting the pithy observation of the course tutor: 'Men, here's a hot tip, first thing upon rising, empty your bowels', or words to that effect. Next day during the official tour of the trenches I was asked to give the points for and against my own dugout.

The course was approaching its end and many were uneasy at the imminent prospect of spending the remainder of the war in the thick of the fighting at the front. They received a further foretaste during instruction in ammunition.

Snipers often moved in No-Man's-Land between the lines. If spotted by the enemy they would be engaged with heavy infantry weapons. In order to judge the correct defensive method, it was an advantage to recognize these weapons by the noise they made when fired. If one came under mortar attack for example, it was only a question of time before the Russians got the range or saturated the area so thoroughly that one could not avoid falling victim. In this case it was essential to leave the trench at once. If one could not retire through cover, the alternative was to jump up suddenly and run in wild zigzags for the German lines. As previously stated, snipers called this the '*Hasensprung*' – the hare's jump. It required a high degree of composure but offered the only possibility of surviving the situation. Hare's leap was therefore practised repeatedly in training, yet when the hour came many snipers preferred to remain in their foxholes in a blue funk, and perished.

While a real mortar could be fired for our instruction, a gramophone record was played for the acoustic demonstration of one of the most feared Soviet weapons, the 'Stalin organ', a multiple rocket launcher mounted on a lorry. The full battery would transform a football field into a blizzard of steel splinters and worked earth. The rhythmic, howling noise of discharge played at full volume made the stomach turn. When my co-trainees asked me what was the best defence, I replied, 'Find the deepest hole possible, and pray.'

To round off, a new kind of infantry ammunition was shown. This was known as the 'B-Patrone' (B-bullet), 'B' standing for '*Beobachtung*' or observation. It had been developed originally as a tracer round for calibrating fighter weapons. The round exploded on impact and indicated the accuracy of the burst. Aerial MG-gunners were able to calibrate their weapons relatively quickly using this optical aid. The ammunition was very expensive, however, and its use limited to the purpose for which it was designed. The Russians, on the other hand, had issued it to their troops from the onset of the Barbarossa campaign. It was much feared by the German infantry because of the terrible wounds it inflicted. Russian snipers were particularly keen on it. I had already had experience of explosive bullets, and to the extent that the enemy had no compunction in putting it into general use I considered it justifiable that German snipers should receive the issue. The munition used in small arms was illegal under the Geneva Convention, but the Russians had obviously waived the right to object and the war was at such a desperate stage for ourselves, having regard to the type of people we faced in the East, that the end practically justified any means. During a short demonstration with these bullets, trees 5cm in diameter were felled without difficulty.

During the last two weeks of instruction, the course concentrated more on the practical. Besides the daily visits to the firing range and the shooting garden, we concentrated on movement in the field, passing unseen through military exercises held by other units, or infiltrating between the lines. Later the principle of the shooting garden was transferred to open terrain and a time limit imposed for spotting and shooting at the papier mâché figures. For failure, points were deducted from the score-card and 'death' awarded. My inexperienced colleagues quickly came to understand the dangers of the life they had embraced. When these drills began, they 'died' like flies, and I was not a stranger to error myself. Yet it was not quite so bad as it looked, for official sniper tactics were permanently offensive while in reality on the battlefield many difficult situations resolved themselves by a healthy dose of caution. A good sniper had to know when it was best to vanish, but the training programme did not teach discretion.

The course concluded on Saturday 1 July 1944 with a celebration party, the CSM having conjured up a few barrels of beer, schnapps and some sides of pig for an outdoor grill. Beforehand our group of sixty fell in to hear their results. Each man was called forward individually, first the four who had failed and were being returned to unit, then those who had passed, beginning in reverse order with the fifty-sixth. After a handshake from the CSM, each man received his personal rifle with optic, a *Wehrpass* bearing the registration number of his 'ZF-Gewehr', a certificate confirming his success and final position in class, and a parchment in Gothic lettering reading:

German Sniper.
Impress upon yourself these ten rules:
1. Fight fanatically! You are a people hunter!
2. Shoot calmly and deliberately, without haste: the hit rewards you!
3. The most deadly opponent is the enemy sniper! Always reckon with him and attempt to outfox him!
4. Never fire more than once from your position!
5. The entrenching tool lengthens your life, trench-digging spares blood!
6. Practise distance estimation constantly.
7. Be a master of camouflage and in use of terrain!
8. Maintain your shooting skills through constant practice even when away from the front!
9. Never let your sniper's rifle out of your hand and give it careful upkeep! A perfectly functioning weapon is your strength and safety!
10. After being wounded, your return to the front is preceded by a fresh sniper's course to sharpen your faculties!
Your goal should be the Sniper's Badge, awarded to the Best.

I finished in second place and so won an ammunition crate full of delicacies wine, cigarettes, chocolate, cold meats and so forth. At least I would not arrive home for leave empty-handed! The act of receiving the rifle with optic made one a sniper officially. Yet while the inexperienced man swelled with pride at his élite status, we veterans looked ahead with foreboding. Most of the course participants were already rattling to the Eastern Front aboard a supply train next day while I went home by lorry. I had given my family brief warning of my arrival, and my parents and sisters were expecting me. Once inside the front door I took my sniper rifle from my shoulder and rested it carefully against the wall. Producing from my rucksack the edible evidence of my success, it was the chocolate wrapped in red tinfoil that really broke the tension of the moment.

My father's workshop had ensured that my family continued well fed. Pressed to reminisce, at the table I related a few anecdotes of a soldier's life at the front, which was, so I assured them, an exciting, sometimes tense adventure spiced with not a little danger at times – in fact the type of life any young man might wish for himself. Afterwards I lay in bed unable to sleep, unable to dislodge the lie stuck in my throat. Next day I helped my father in the workshop to take my mind off the war. We worked in silent harmony – he had served as a *Gebirgsjäger* in the Austro-Hungarian Army during the Great War and understood my mood. He had gone to war rejoicing, only for its iron fist to crush his spirit. He returned home years later a sober, wiser man.

The few days in the bosom of my family flew by. Friends and school classmates were absent, all either in the *Wehrmacht*, or fallen for Greater Germany: our village families looked towards an uncertain future. The controlled Press spoke in terms of eventual victory, but all could read between the lines. A new term, 'an elastic command policy on all fronts' could only mean retreat. The Western Allies, now radiating out from Normandy, were encroaching towards the Reich from France in the west and Italy in the south: in the east the Russians had unwrapped a massive offensive against Army Group Centre. Within the last four weeks the pressure on the German armies had intensified beyond the point where there was any hope of withstanding it.

On 13 July 1944 my father offered me his hand in farewell, his face carved in stone. My mother and sisters had dissolved in tears and were lost for words. Resolutely I turned towards the east. It was all now in the hands of the fates.

Chapter 9

Rumania, August 1944:
The Stab in the Back

In a way it was a relief to get back to the Rumanian front. During my leave I saw a world at peace where there was none. I had become estranged from civilian life. At the front I knew what had to be done. My company, my regiment – these were the family and the road, if necessary to the bitter end.

At the terminus of the line I alighted together with seven travelling companions. An Opel Blitz lorry was waiting at the station for dispatches and gave us a lift to battalion HQ at a place called Bistritz. I knew the driver. Alois was a long-serving NCO who kept his ear to the ground. He told me something was brewing. When he fetched the regimental commander, I overheard talk about a Hungarian intelligence report. The Russians were preparing a major offensive and it was reported that our Rumanian ally was ready to defect. Army Group Centre had come under pressure and 6.Army, which held the line together, was threatened with encirclement. Alois drew out a bottle of Ostler from beneath the driving seat. We drank directly from the neck. The journey continued thus, snatches of conversation interspersed with drink. I could tell that something wasn't right. Alois gabbled about the summer weather they had been having, a nice relationship with the adjoining Rumanian frontier unit, and about personnel and material supplies which had brought the regiment almost back to strength.

When we finally reached battalion HQ, he invited me to meet the Rumanian frontier infantry that evening. Occasionally there were girls there, apparently all I needed was charm and a gift of black bread and they would be putty in my hands. I promised to think about it – duty came first. I reported my return from leave to the CSM of the battalion staff company. *Hauptmann* Kloss was in the room and seemed genuinely pleased to see me. 'You've come just at the right time. We need every good man we can lay our hands on,' he said. He joked about the 'harshness' of the course having made 'a good sniper' of me, and then suddenly warned that within a few days, Ivan was going to turn us into Christmas stuffing. 'And another thing,' he added, 'the Rumanians are up to no good. I fear they may change sides. The regimental staff received a telex from Foreign Armies East which reported Hungarian sources at the highest level as saying a Rumanian resistance group has been formed. Apparently they are negotiating with the Russians. OKH is not convinced but personally I think there is something in it. So, do me a favour and stay clear of the Rumanians.' He shuffled through a sheaf of papers and produced a certificate and a small item wrapped in brown paper, which he passed to me, offering his hand with the observation, 'I congratulate you on being awarded the infantry assault badge.' He slapped my back and sat at his desk. 'Have a look round first. Then we'll talk again tomorrow.'

Shouldering my rifle and pack I wandered through the despatch runners' bunker looking for familiar faces. To my dismay I found few, a mere sprinkling among the new arrivals, half of whom would not survive the coming offensive. At the end of my rounds I called in on the regimental armourer. My first question was naturally about the young sniper to whom my Russian sniper-rifle had been entrusted.

'That young man met a bad end,' the sergeant replied gravely. 'It was fairly quiet here in the last couple of weeks, just the odd reconnaissance sortie – you know the drill, have a snoop round, bring back a prisoner for questioning and so on, convince them we're still up for it. Anyway, he went out alone on the hunt too soon. We don't know exactly what happened except that he failed to return at the appointed time that evening. Four days later one of the patrols found his body, swollen like a balloon in the heat. He must have fallen into their hands and failed to get rid of his rifle in time.' He shook his head as he reflected on the horror he was about to convey. 'Can you imagine what Ivan does to a sniper whom he finds in possession of a Russian rifle with loads of notches on the stock? The corpse was green and blue with a thousand knife cuts. Finally they cut off his balls and stuffed them in his mouth. Then they rammed the barrel of the rifle up his rectum as far as the back sight. His death must have been sheer hell. The boys who found him in No-Man's-Land buried him straight away. When they got back and recovered they were all for going out again to take revenge.' He paused for breath and continued, 'Sepp, can you imagine what it's going to be like when these rapists and murderers get to the Reich?' Laying a fatherly hand on my shoulder, he stared me in the eye earnestly. 'We're fighting for survival, to the last bullet, and when that's gone, to the last entrenching tool.'

Death was routine and the incident did not disturb me particularly although in the light of the atrocity I decided to abandon the practice of notching up each kill on the rifle stock and considered how to remove every outward sign that I was a sniper.

The pressure from the north on the Carpathian Front was growing ever stronger. 3.G.D. commanders were doing whatever possible to strengthen their overstretched sector. The Rumanians were integrated into our defensive line. In early August the Soviets initiated their first systematic nuisance raids, and on 19 August 1944 laid an artillery barrage on neighbouring G.J.R. 138 prior to an assault. The Rumanians put up no resistance and were flattened – G.J.R. 138 was pincered. They fought desperately to break free, and the few reserves at division were thrown hastily and at considerable strategic risk into the fray. After four days of bitter fighting the encirclement crumbled and the front line restabilized. My battalion, II./144 was not involved and had only a few skirmishes.

Almost every night I went out on patrol in No-Man's-Land. I often noticed small enemy groups disappear into the Rumanian lines. Significantly this was never followed by any sounds of fighting. By the third day when I was sure there was a conspiracy afoot, I reported my observations to the battalion commander. 'Shit,' Kloss said, 'so there is something in the rumours after all. Sepp, it will happen, you'll see – the Rumanians are going to stab us in the back.'

Ignoring the reports of their commanders on the spot, OKH remained unimpressed by claims that Rumania was about to defect from the Axis. It is difficult to understand how they can have arrived at the contrary conclusion, for a host of pointers had indicated a change in sentiment on the part of the Rumanians from the summer of 1944 onwards. Pro-German commanders had been replaced by anti-German, and the flow of information to German command centres had slackened noticeably and taken on a contradictory nature. Inadequately armed, equipped and supplied, Rumanian troops had taken extremely heavy losses on the Eastern Front, were burnt out and far more war-weary than their German allies. The Russian invasion of their country was imminent and they felt helpless to do anything to prevent it. When the Russian offensive against Army Group Ukraine South began with the objective of encircling 6.Army, two Rumanian armies defending the southern flank were overrun in a single day and night and put to flight in disorder. Since Stalingrad, the Rumanian monarch and opposition parties had been negotiating a separate peace treaty in secret with the Soviets, but the terms were so drastic that no agreement had been possible. Since June 1944, however, Rumania had edged closer under the impetus of their own communist faction.

A plan to break with Germany coinciding with the Russian offensive against Army Group South had been drawn up, and on 23 August 1944, in realistic acceptance of the hopelessness of the situation and the threat to Rumania's borders, the Rumanian king assented to an armistice and switched his allegiance. That same evening Rumanian forces were ordered to cease hostilities against the Soviet Union forthwith and to pin down German forces in order to prevent their resisting the Russian attack.

The changeover had immediate effect. The German ambassador and High Command in Rumania were informed that, contrary to the terms of the Rumanian–Russian treaty, the *Wehrmacht* would be permitted to withdraw all its forces, weapons and equipment free of attack provided the Germans left at once. Hitler dismissed the offer out of hand and ordered hostilities to be commenced against Rumania, a fatal error in view of the plight of 6.Army for he now had a war on two fronts locally, which was bound to result in heavy losses in men and material. These could not be replaced and would lead to a complete breakdown. By 30 August, Army Group Ukraine South had been virtually wiped out, a third Stalingrad for the German Army in terms of its losses.

3.G.D. now had an additional enemy to the Russians for the Rumanian people had split into two factions: those who supported the change, future partisans against the *Wehrmacht*; and those who remained loyal to the Axis and continued to side with the Germans as military or refugees.

The Rumanian–Russian pact of 23 August 1944 was concluded on a fine day of high summer. Our regiment had anxieties about the situation of 6.Army and Army Group Ukraine South to the north of us, but G.J.R. 144 lay along a peaceful sector of the front with no enemy presence. At midday at battalion HQ I met Alois the lorry driver who was about to make a courier run. He renewed his invitation to me to socialize with the neighbouring Rumanian unit that evening, remarking that drink would be freely available, and so I agreed to come. Alois told me how to get there and called from his cab window in parting, 'See you at eight, don't get shot dead in the meantime.'

It was shortly before nine that evening, sniper rifle at my shoulder, that I made my way through thick woodland towards the meeting place. Although 2 kilometres behind the front line, I maintained a constant awareness of my surroundings, an innate faculty that had often saved my bacon. I had reached the bend in the path, which descended into the Rumanian positions, when I heard some odd noises – very excited, raised voices, and suppressed cries and groans which filled the still air of that warm evening. I disappeared at once into the undergrowth. About 50 metres from the bend was a small elevation which provided a view of the Rumanian position, and peering through thick bush at the summit I found myself looking down into a valley bottom about the size of a football field where the Rumanian border troops were dug in.

Through my binoculars I saw five *Jäger*, one of whom was Alois, at the end of the woodland path about 100 metres away surrounded by Rumanians and two Russians. The Germans were bound and about to be interrogated. For this purpose there was a Rumanian interpreter who relayed the questions of the Russians to the German prisoners. The answers were apparently unsatisfactory, for one of the Soviets pushed the interpreter aside and began to jab at the *Jäger*'s face with a rifle butt. A group of Rumanians were standing around the scene and I could see by their expressions that they did not approve. Next, a Rumanian officer appeared and remonstrated with his men. This had no apparent effect until he drew a pistol, which motivated the NCOs in the group to drive the remainder back to their positions. The officer then appeared to suggest to the inquisitors that they should conduct the proceedings in a less exposed area. At the foot of the slope to the right of my hiding place was the latrine block, and the prisoners were led behind the weather-boarded rear wall out of sight of the compound, which was better for me. The distance was about 80 metres. The five German prisoners were in the hands of two Russians and two Rumanians plus the interpreter. The captors decided to concentrate on Alois, and after a few violent kicks, punches and more jabs with the rifle butt he collapsed to the ground. They untied his wrists, dragged him to the latrine wall and spread his left hand on a ledge. The Russian leader withdrew a pistol from its holster and smashed the stock down on Alois' outstretched fingertips. Alois screamed in a mixture of rage and pain. I felt a wild urge to take action, but suppressed it: I had to wait for the right moment. A hasty reaction could be fatal for us all and in any case, I had to report the changed situation regarding the Rumanians to battalion HQ. I could not do this if I was dead or captured. Therefore I bided my time and considered feverishly how best to help my five colleagues, hoping that the other side would see sense and simply take them off as prisoners of war.

In order to silence his cries, Alois was gagged. His suffering was obviously the example to the others to reveal whatever it was that the inquisitors wished to know. Despite the encouragement of beatings, they failed to provide the required information, and so the fingertips of Alois' right hand received the same treatment as the left. As he writhed in agony, the questioning of the other four was resumed. I had prepared a rest for the barrel of my rifle and positioned it to my satisfaction. As I watched, the Soviet torturer ripped open Alois' tunic and trousers, took out a pocket knife and opened it, then waved it threateningly in the faces of the four kneeling German soldiers. After some shouting and yelling, the Rumanian interpreter shrugged his shoulders in resignation. At this the Russian bent down to Alois, slit open his abdomen and through the wound brought out about a metre's length of intestine. Alois' screams of pain were audible despite the gag. I had seen many terrible sights in this war, but this was the worst to date, and it had gone far enough. The situation was too much for the Rumanian interpreter, for he drew his pistol and put Alois out of his suffering with two quick shots to the head. At this a shouting match broke out at the latrine between the Russians and the Rumanians. Both Russians drew their pistols. The four German survivors, hands bound behind their backs looked on, eyes large in panic, from their enforced kneeling position. The Russian torturer threatened the Rumanian interpreter with the pistol, then aimed it at the nearest German prisoner and shot him in the face. The lifeless body remained kneeling upright for a few moments before toppling sideways.

The important thing for a sniper in such a situation is to control his emotions. The two Russians had to be killed, not in rage, but professionally. I took the first Russian in my sights, held my breath, concentrated calmly, took up pressure on the trigger and pulled smoothly. The bullet tore through the chest of the target and threw him backwards like a rag doll. The second looked around in surprise: his face came into my sights and I fired. Two dead. The main job was completed. The Rumanian interpreter had quickly sized up the problem and cleared the chest-high latrine wall like an Olympic high jumper, his fall broken by the trench of semi-solids on the far side. Instead of taking cover the other two Rumanians fired off wild MP bursts towards the woods, nowhere near me, and presented no danger. My third shot catapulted one of them against the latrine wall. By now the compound was in uproar. Covered in faeces from head to toe, the interpreter was running from the foul trench into which he had fallen. An MG gave him covering fire, the projectiles whistling too close for comfort. I could do nothing further for the surviving three *Jäger*; it was my duty to raise the alarm. Like a ghost I vanished into the forest, avoiding the pathways and moving through the bushes. When I reached II./144 HQ it was already a hive of activity. I was admitted at once to the commander's office and reported in brief sentences. Although I omitted the details, it was obvious to Kloss what had occurred.

'Damn,' was all he said, and in great excitement attempted to telephone regimental HQ at Borca, 10 kilometres north, and neighbouring units. Kloss was already in receipt of information that Rumanian units integrated into the German defensive system had turned on adjoining companies and taken prisoners. My report provided the final confirmation that Rumania was an enemy.

Regimental HQ was clearly taken aback and had nothing to recommend, promising only to have the situation clarified at divisional HQ. Kloss managed to warn III./144 of G.A.R. before the telephone network was sabotaged. Each unit was now cut off and forced to act independently as had happened so frequently in recent months. Our battalion had been lucky this time. Forewarned, runners were sent out to all companies of II./144 alerting them to the danger, and no Rumanian ruse succeeded.

Many others suffered severe losses from Rumanian treachery. Their troops would approach our unsuspecting positions with outward friendliness, then open fire without warning. Partisan-type fighting groups were built up around a nucleus of Russian agents and encouraged to strike with the utmost brutality. This caused panic in our lines, for it was impossible to know the difference between friend and foe. One of these partisan outfits approached II./144 with their customary smiles and waves, their weapons not slung from the shoulder, but carried baby-fashion in the arms: we shot them down to the last man the instant they made their move.

The overall position became very precarious with the onset of nightfall. Although the Rumanians lacked heavy infantry weapons, their numbers could wear us down. In these difficult hours G.J.R. 144 became the backbone of 3.G.D. resistance and the hub of its reorganization. Survivors from far-flung companies fought through to the regiment to swell its numbers, and next morning hastily-formed regimental assault units, inspired by rage and indignation at the treachery of their former ally, went on a berserk drive for revenge. No prisoners were taken, and even if we had wanted to, the Rumanians had destroyed the logistical situation.

I accompanied one such group. The carbine with optical sight interfered with movement during search and destroy missions of this kind. On my return from leave I had discovered that the regiment had a small stock of Modell 43 semi-automatic rifles, and after trying out a couple had selected the best, which the weapons and supply NCO guarded with his life. Using explosive rounds over distances up to 100 metres, its performance was awesome. Within a few days the general area was cleared of Rumanian troops and the front stabilized.

At the same time, 6.Army to our north was being slaughtered while the Russians had besieged Bucharest and the Ploesti oilfields in the south of the country. 3.G.D. projected into the Russian Front like a thorn, and it took no great stretch of the imagination to see that once they had mopped us to the north, we were next on their shopping list. Our front extended for 30 kilometres from the Aurel Pass (*Gruppe* Lorch, I./144 and III./144) to the town of Bistricidara (in German Bistritz – *Gruppe* Mecklenburg, II./144). On 27 August 1944 the Russians attacked along this broad front, and within a few days their offensive had taken under fire all Carpathian passes to the Siebenbürgen tableland held by 3.G.D.

II./144 was of special importance and used as a 'fire-fighting' unit, deployed to every hotspot as it came under pressure and forcing open dangerous encirclements to allow trapped companies to escape. Used generally as infantry but trained as mountain troops, our regiment operated over terrain it knew well and had the tactical edge over the Russians. On the other hand we were outnumbered by twenty to one and however well we fought the writing was on the wall.

One of our units had become trapped between Russians and Rumanians in a Carpathian mountain pass. An assault platoon had been formed to relieve it and I came along as sniper escort. The Rumanians were ten strong, armed with a heavy machine-gun and rifles. They were inferior to the German force but had a good field of fire from well dug-in positions. Overall they must have been very confident of their own safety. We were favoured by thick woodland for our approach, but were unacquainted with the patch of terrain around which the Rumanians were lodged.

The platoon sergeant and I made an observation of the enemy group through field glasses and drew some comfort from the fact that our arrival had not been detected, giving us the decisive element of surprise. We fell upon our erstwhile ally like a rainstorm from a cloudless sky. Hand-grenades followed by bursts of MP-fire and single, accurate sniper rounds transformed their safe position within seconds into a simmering witches' cauldron from which there was no escape.

The problem of the German unit ahead was not solved by the eradication of the Rumanians, for to retreat they required to cross an open plain 100 metres or so in length, overlooked by the Russians and within range of their weapons. At first they must have been dismayed to hear the sound of battle at their backs, then overjoyed to see the field-grey uniforms of their relief. I watched their excited conversation and gestures through binoculars. As we tried to envisage a way out of the predicament, a heavy mortar opened up. The Soviets had obviously called up heavy weapons to remove the obstruction to their passage through the pass. The men of the trapped unit threw themselves down as the bombs hissed over. The salvo was aimed at the forward defensive position and fell short. With dull explosions it churned up the earth. Each succeeding salvo fell nearer and nearer yet. Through binoculars I saw their panic-stricken faces. We were condemned to inactivity, and the defenders' only chance to escape being blown to shreds was a long dash across open country. Shortly before the first mortars exploded in the main positions, the occupants had jumped up and run pell-mell towards us. They were picked off one by one with rifle fire, for instead of running in wild zigzags, they tried to make the edge of the wood by sprinting in a straight line. I recognized at once the handiwork of a Russian sniper armed with a semi-automatic. I had seen examples of the Tokarev 40 and had even tested a captured specimen for myself. Although not as accurate as the Walther 43, its action was more reliable and gave the experienced sharpshooter a much increased rate of fire. Our armourer had told me that there was a sniper version on issue with the same optic as I had used at the start of my career.

The Russian mortar teams now turned their attention to the position on a wooded slope, hacking the wounded to shreds and burying their remains under the wreckage of the forest and large clumps of earth. A sudden stillness descended over the area, broken only by the cries of the wounded on the open plain. Two men volunteered for a rescue mission. This seemed to me to be highly unwise. Cautiously using the sparse and inadequate cover, they worked their way to their wounded comrades of the other unit. When they reached the first casualty, helper number one raised him to inspect the wound. A shot whipped across the slope and bored a fist-sized hole in the helper's chest. Blood sprayed out from the wound like a fountain. Apparently the explosive round had severed an artery. The body trembled a little and then collapsed in death. With my binoculars I swept the distant woods in an effort to identify the Russian positions but they were well hidden and too far off for our weapons. The presence of the Russian sniper made any further attempt at rescue impossible, and helper number two was very fortunate to make it back in one piece. The shouts and cries of the seriously wounded ebbed away until death extinguished them. The exception was a *Jäger* with a kidney wound that was not fatal. He gave vent to his terrible agony with primeval cries interrupted only by short periods of unconsciousness. He was begging us to come for him, but it could not be done without sacrificing more lives.

The cries died down and a terrible groan for help rent the stillness. The man raised an arm imploringly, the fingers of his hand spread. Seconds later an explosive bullet from the Russian sniper hit the hand, which broke at the wrist and hung down uselessly, still connected by a few tendons, dangling like a broken branch. The bones of the forearm were now exposed to the elements. The Russians obviously wanted to teach us how the Russian hero fought.

The terrible cries and screams began again. My platoon sergeant summoned me. Placing a hand on my shoulder and looking at me with his grave eyes he said, 'I can't order you, only plead. I know it's asking a lot, but I urge you please to put that poor man out of his suffering with a clean shot. You are the only person here who can do it with a rifle at this distance.'

104

This was the situation I had feared I would have to confront some day. I had often looked on as the Russians killed their own wounded in inaccessible regions of the battlefield. But on the German side this was uncommon, for the systematic disposal of the wounded in this manner cheapened life and demoralized the troops. It was an unwritten law of the *Gebirgsjäger* to bring in the wounded if humanly possible. The only exception was killing at the sufferer's request in a hopeless situation. In months gone by I had shuddered to watch as wounded soldiers capable of surviving but incapable of being transported out had begged a comrade to render the *coup de grâce* to spare them further suffering. It was customary for the Russians to kill off enemy wounded, the reason being, so it has been subsequently explained, that the medical infrastructure was not in place. They were, however, at a loss to explain why it was also necessary for them to torture the wounded before delivering the final shot.

This man was not mortally wounded and I vacillated, but my colleagues urged me on: 'Come on man, do it. For God's sake put the poor bastard out of his misery.' Reluctantly, beset by scruple, I laid my carbine on a rolled-up tent as a rest. The range was less than 80 metres, but the head of the target was occasionally hidden by grass as he writhed and the body lay behind a slight inundation. I loaded an explosive bullet, aimed towards where I had seen the head and awaited my opportunity. Suddenly his body froze in a spasm of agony, the cries rang out hoarse, the head appeared. I aimed at the ear, pulled the trigger and saw the head burst open. A silence fell over the plain.

The Russians went to ground. Apparently this development had stunned them and they had returned to their holes in bewilderment. It gave us time to beat a hasty retreat. We made our way back to battalion in silence, not even exchanging glances. Dumb, sunk in thought, each man was glad that he had not been called upon to do the deed. One may call it an act of mercy, but to this very day I am plagued with guilt by this minor episode.

A few days later I was sniper escort to another assault platoon sent out to visit a German unit that was overdue. On the way we had to cross a Russian minefield through which an engineer company had cleared a narrow track marked by little flags the previous day. We were not all that confident about this track, and tip-toed through it with bated breath. It took ninety minutes to get across, after which we entered some bushy country. The veterans of the platoon had developed a sixth sense for terrain and danger, and after a further kilometre or so the advance party discovered another minefield, this one fitted with neat little trip wires. This would be the flank protection for Soviet positions nearby. Cautiously, using all available cover, we attempted to circumnavigate it, but this intention was more problematical and time-consuming than we first thought. When dusk fell we were forced to turn back since movement in mined terrain by night was very dangerous. Before doing so the platoon sergeant had become curious to know what could be seen from the top of a nearby hill and asked me to accompany him. To our surprise it gave a panoramic view of some very sturdy looking Russian positions. While examining these through field glasses, about 20 metres to one end of them I noticed a movement in the bushes and saw a small patch of a light shade appear. On closer inspection I realized I was looking at a Russian crouching at the toilet.

The sergeant whispered, 'Sepp, do you see that Ivan over there having a shit? If you put one in him, you'll give them a fright. They think we're all somewhere else. I'll go back with the others. Hold back your shot as long as possible and then follow.' At that he disappeared, leaving me to take the Russian in the crosswires of my optic. The range was at least 150 metres. To be sure of a breast shot I aimed at his throat, took a deep breath, concentrated briefly, then fired. At that moment the Russian rose, and the projectile passed through his lower abdomen, leaving a hole the size of a fist. He collapsed screaming in pain and panic. Appalled, his friends poured out of their underground shelter and fired wildly into the night. I reversed out of my hilltop lair and hastened to rejoin my platoon.

Next morning the same platoon was again outward bound on the mission to find the lost unit. Additionally we had to capture a prisoner and bring him back for questioning about enemy positions and movements. We used the same route as the previous day. A similar idea had occurred to the Russians, but they had left later and our paths crossed just ahead of their lines. Since we always exercised more caution than they did, we spotted them earlier and so gained the element of surprise. A further advantage was that our platoon was equipped with a new rifle, which had been delivered to the front in small quantities over the last few weeks. The Sturmgewehr 44 was a cross between a machine-pistol and a carbine. A lever allowed a choice between semi-automatic and automatic fire. Ammunition was a shorter version of the Pistolenpatrone 43 carbine bullet. The magazine held thirty rounds. The ammunition was effective at up to 300 metres and the weapon was much better in use than the Mauser K98k carbine because the force was weaker and some of the recoil energy was diverted to the automatic reload mechanism. The powerful recoil of the standard carbine resulted in severe bruising to the shoulder after forty or so rounds. This was the reason why the carbine was so inaccurate in use – because of the unpleasant recoil, fire was widely dispersed.

In a short, violent exchange with the Russian patrol, the Sturmgewehr proved itself an excellent new acquisition. Within a few minutes we had shot the lot with no losses, the only survivors being non-transportable severely wounded cases. We had become less soft-hearted in recent days and a *Jäger* humane killer did the rounds of the Russian wounded. Unlike the Russians, we saw no need to interfere with the wound before administering the final shot. The Russian corpses were searched for valuable documents such as paybooks, ID papers and cards bearing tactical insignia. After a few minutes the Russian position opened up with heavy mortars and we were forced to sprint along the edge of their fancy minefield, which we had discovered the previous day. Beyond lay bushy upland. A couple of hundred metres inside it we came upon the German position we had been looking for and, as expected, found them all dead. From the looks of it they had fought until all ammunition was expended and then been butchered in hand-to-hand fighting with Russians and Rumanians. From amidst the bushes we could look down into the shallow valley, strewn with German dead. We could go no closer, however, for there was little cover, and enemy positions not being far away we had to reckon with a revenge raid coming soon, suspicious noises already being reported.

Searching the terrain through binoculars, my eyes fell on a grenade crater about 20 metres off. My attention was arrested by a brand-new *Jäger* peaked cap, its tin-plated edelweiss insignia glinting in the sunshine. I decided that this would make a handsome replacement for my own ragged, filthy cap. I crept closer with caution and was only a few metres short of the crater when I saw the dead soldier. Multiple splinters had turned his upper torso into a bloody mash through which his ribs showed. Hundreds of flies buzzed round the decaying corpse. His ID chain had rucked up around his ears, the tags near his head. When the grenade exploded it must have blown the cap undamaged from his head. Once at his side, I placed my old cap over his face and tried the new one for size. It was a perfect fit. At that moment I heard a vehicle approaching and decided it was high time to disappear. I did think of taking the ID tags with me but got distracted. Once in the bush I intended to return for them but the Russian vehicle prevented my fulfilling the intention. The dead German soldier, whoever he was, disappeared into the lists of the missing. Just a moment on my part and his family would have known his fate for sure. But I was selfish, and saw only the cap. Those unredeemed ID tags were the evidence of my personal failing.

Within a few days the flames of war flared in all Rumania. Russian units besieged Bucharest and headed for the important Ploesti oilfields, which had kept the German war machine going for so long. Like a rock in the surf, the Carpathian strongholds of 3.G.D. blocked the Red Army's way to the Siebenbürgen plain. It was hardly surprising therefore that the Soviets should respond with everything to hand. They were met with ambush strategy. Intent on forcing the valleys, they encountered delaying tactics in which snipers thrived. In well-camouflaged positions we waited for them to reach a certain point and then engaged. Even with numerically inferior forces we enjoyed a long period of success simply because the Russians could not develop their attack strategy while confined to mountain passes, under fire and taking heavy losses in men and material. On average I fired twenty aimed rounds per day, and only a few of these kills ever found their way into the official tallies.

It was in early September 1944 that *Hauptmann* Kloss showed me an OKH circular affecting Army and *Waffen*-SS snipers. By order of the Führer, a special Sniper Badge in three award grades had been introduced. The first grade was for twenty, the second with silver cord trim for forty and the third, with gold cord trim, for sixty confirmed kills. The new field-grey oval cloth badge, featuring a black raven's head above three oak leaves inside the coloured cord trim, was to be worn on the lower right sleeve of the uniform jacket above any additional trade badge. It went without saying that no sniper in his right mind would ever wear this badge at the front. The silver strips, which few wore, were dangerous enough, and the meaning of an official badge would soon have come to the enemy's attention. It would have been suicidal to wear such an advertisement.

As before, all kills in straightforward attack and defence were not to count. At the instigation of the *Reichsführer*-SS, in this connection all previous confirmed kills were to be sacrificed to the Führer, and on the appointed date all tallies were to begin afresh from zero. So that the sniper should not be left empty-handed, he was to be recompensed for his kills to date with the award of the Iron Cross Second Class (EK II) or, if he already had one, the Iron Cross First Class (EK I). A few days later I received the EK II.

In this official elevation of the formerly despised German sniper, it was possible to discern an armaments objective. To motivate the fanatical lone warrior who, armed with only a rifle, could replace an artillery battery, was very cost effective, and to some extent might compensate the ever more catastrophic shortfall in weapons and equipment.

Chapter 10

Into Hungary: The Soviet Liberators as I Came to Know Them

While the Soviets persevered without success against 3.G.D. strongholds in the Carpathian mountains of Rumania, they had managed to invest Hungary by another route and now threatened the division with a fresh encirclement. There was nothing for it but to abandon our positions and retreat to the Maros river on the Siebenbürgen plain. This meant fighting westward over 200 kilometres to get there. We marched at night and by day fought off the Russians, who were able to attack not only from the rear but also on the flank. When we marched, my battalion commander *Hauptmann* Kloss would go ahead to identify suitable locations to stop the following day. He would always ask me to accompany him, since Kloss considered me to be a battle-hardened veteran with nerves of steel and could rely on me unconditionally. I was therefore also his body-guard. As a career officer, Kloss had learnt horse-riding as a matter of course. On the Eastern Front a horse enabled its rider to traverse trackless terrain quickly and silently, and thus Kloss rode daily. As his bodyguard I was given a tough little steppe-horse. I had never ridden in my life but a colleague who had been a farmer and horse owner pre-war taught me the essentials in my spare time over a one-week period. From 1943 onward, the Germany Army in the East relied on hundreds of thousands of horses for logistical purposes. The horse guaranteed a certain basic mobility, for shortages of fuel and spare parts combined with heavy losses in motor vehicles had hit us hard. Some infantry units had no vehicles whatsoever. The plentiful numbers of Eastern European horses known collectively as '*Panjepferde*' or steppe-horses became the indispensable support of German troops during the great retreat.

I was knocked unconscious during the early stages of the march into Hungary. We had overtaken an infantry unit which had two battle-worthy SP-guns. The officer reported that a patrol had seen a column of Russian tanks ahead. I was riding pillion on a motorcycle combination with *Hauptmann* Kloss in the sidecar when, level with the muzzle of the leading SP-gun no more than 2 metres away, the machine stopped abruptly and fired. I was blinded by the flash and tossed, presumably by the muzzle pressure wave, into a hedgerow skirting the highway, where I lost consciousness. When I came to, I saw the motorcycle rider rolling on the ground while Kloss was still in the sidecar, evidently concussed. The fire-fight with the Russian tanks was short-lived and help arrived swiftly, but it was days before I lost the whistling in my ears.

Before reaching our new defensive line in Hungary, one night we passed through a wooded valley along the Maros river in search of a suitable daytime stopping place. I was trotting ahead of my company. They were all chronically overtired and were plodding along as if in a trance. Only the security platoon, of which I formed part, was really alert. A five-man advance party was leading about 50 metres ahead. Suddenly a dull detonation awoke everyone from his lethargy, and I saw one of the leading group fall to the ground and set off another explosion. I realized at once that he had stepped on a mine. Since there was no firing it was not an ambush.

The order was passed down the line that nobody should move except with the utmost caution. Being well forward, I worked towards the wounded man together with a medic. In the light of a flashlamp we saw a face pallid with shock. The initial explosion had blown off his left leg below the knee, and when he fell he had sat on the second mine, which detonated, inflicting corresponding injuries. Nothing could be done for him, and he bled to death. Ritual had no place on this front. The dead man was a material loss, a statistic, and he was left where he fell. The medic retrieved his ID tags, the company lined up in Indian file well behind two engineers on their hands and knees who probed the ground with a bayonet for more mines. We established later that we had stumbled into a minefield laid by Hungarian troops to cover their retreat from the Russians. It took five hours to progress a few hundred metres, but eventually we came out without further losses. In general, German soldiers did not encounter mined areas very often. Since as a rule we were in constant retreat, it was mainly the Russians who ran up against the problem.

At dawn we reached our new temporary location and dug in. The Russians were on our heels and we expected the first reconnaissance patrols at any moment. I was accompanying the battalion commander on an informal inspection tour of the bunkers when suddenly a single rifle shot rang out and broke the morning stillness. It hit an MG position about 5 metres ahead. Kloss and I reached the trench bent double and found a young *Jäger* sitting holding a field cap from which the edelweiss insignia had been ripped off. I knew the cause immediately – a Russian sniper. The MG-gunner, only a few days at the front, saw *Hauptmann* Kloss and, intending to explain where the shot had come from, stood up and pointed. Before he had time to speak I launched myself at him like a football goalkeeper to drag him down, but in the same second the sniper fired again, the shot glancing off the boy's head, opening a fearful wound. He had not lost consciousness but suffered brain damage. We bandaged him until his head looked like a white pumpkin, then stretchered the casualty to battalion HQ where he asked over and over, 'What happened? Have I been hurt?'

When he reverted to talking as a young child, Kloss wrapped a fatherly arm around the boy and said, 'You just stay quiet, son. You've had an accident. We're going home soon, and then everything will be all right.'

I stayed to keep the boy company. The word spread quickly that a Russian sniper had infiltrated No-Man's-Land, and that great caution was necessary. It was expected that *Obergefreiter* Allerberger would cure the problem. As was the case with only a few other soldiers, the sniper was the man of whom the others had constant expectations. The officers especially demanded unlimited zealous commitment in the execution of orders that were often beyond the bounds of possibility. If the sniper achieved what he had been sent out to do, he had done no more than his duty. If he failed, he could be condemned as incompetent, or even cowardly. But a sniper could not perform miracles, especially when facing his opposite number. I was fortunate to have had superiors of a mostly generous outlook in this respect.

Whenever possible upon arriving at a new location I would erect a well-camouflaged hide first thing. Once I had been relieved at battalion HQ beside the patient, I occupied the observation post hoping to spot the Russian sniper, but the sly old fox had vanished. I spent all day in tense watchfulness, but only in the evening, as we abandoned the position leaving behind only a small rearguard, did the Russians reveal their presence with a few bursts of MG-fire to see us off.

Hardly had we reached our new positions near Deda on 24 September 1944 than the Russians launched a massive offensive which did not peter out until 8 October, when they broke through the front to the south of 3.G.D. and threatened encirclement. Our division was forced to relinquish its trenches, held at very high cost in lives, and set out for a new front line along the banks of the Theiss river.

The overall situation had deteriorated in the face of political polarization in Hungary. Parts of the Hungarian armed forces were already defecting to the Russians, although a great part remained unconditionally loyal to its Axis partner. For the first time too we became embroiled in large-scale civilian evacuations, and these were not only persons of German stock from the Siebenbürgen, but also anti-communist groups attaching themselves to the retreating *Wehrmacht*. The risk they were running was obviously enormous. The retreat now began to assume an aspect indigestible even for the most hardened *Jäger* stomach.

On the huge Hungarian plain known as the Pussta, vastly superior Russian tank armies flooded to the offensive. In order to retain contact with the main German force, *Armee Gruppe* Woehler, of which 3.G.D. formed part, had to spearhead a way through the Russian attack in order to reach the town of Nyiregyhaza. The stream of refugees became entangled in the bitter fighting. As the political change in Hungary was only half-hearted, the invading Red Army considered themselves victors in enemy territory and provided the civilian population and German forces with a diabolical foretaste of what they could expect once they reached the Reich, and perpetrated the most horrific atrocities. The discovery of the tortured and mutilated bodies of German soldiers was by then of course almost routine. The claim that the Soviet Union was engaged in a life-or-death struggle against fascism, and that anything was justified as a means to an end, even raping Hungarian little girls, has been the alibi acceptable to the former Western Allies in glossing over the crimes of Russian soldiers against civilians in all countries of Eastern Europe during the Second World War. The depths of bestiality and depravity to which the majority of Russian soldiery was allowed to degenerate by its leaders, political and military, is an amazing phenomenon in that, in contrast to the millions of words written about National Socialism, no academic historian has ever written a book about it.

Russian tank units had passed through a small village near Nyiregyhaza and kept going. Subsequently, a company of Russian infantry had occupied the village. When the *Gebirgsjäger* closed in, there was a brief and violent fire-fight decided in our favour, resulting in the survivors of the Russian company withdrawing with heavy losses. On taking possession of the village we noticed that the inhabitants were reticent to show themselves from their cellars and hiding places. Once sure that the Russians had been driven off, they came out to embrace us with a gratitude that was almost pathetic. Upon examination of the houses, the reason for their emotion became clear. We found that the Russians had left a trail of raped women and small girls, the menfolk who protested having been bayoneted or shot. With two colleagues I came upon a distraught and hysterical old man who could not be calmed and kept pointing to a kind of wine cellar. We were naturally concerned that enemy soldiers might be hiding there and surrounded the building. When nobody responded to our demands for the occupants to come out and show themselves, an infantryman drew a stick grenade from his belt, intending to lob it inside. The old man stopped him, clutching his arm and crying. Gesticulating wildly he pushed the German soldier forward into the interior. Hardly had the *Jäger* set foot inside than he backed off, green in the face, leant against a wall for support and vomited. I peered inside the room. What I saw made me gasp in horror. On the floor lay a woman who had been in the last stages of pregnancy. Her abdomen had been slit open with a knife and the foetus extracted. She had bled to death. The foetus had been impaled to a beam with a bayonet. I released the dead child and, having wrapped it with its dead mother in tent-cloth, carried them into the garden, dug a grave and buried them.

Two days later our regiment had advanced to within artillery range of the town of Nyiregyhaza. While our troops waited to open the artillery barrage, I decided to use the time to reconnoitre. I slept for a couple of hours and went out before dawn. After a brief time I came to the first houses on the outskirts of town and slunk cautiously through the gardens and battered ruins. The area had an abandoned look even though it was under Soviet control. The new day dawned and I realized my imprudence in exposing myself to a possible concealed observation post. Slipping from cover to cover, I heard vehicles approaching. It was about seven thirty, and I ought to have been on my way back but I was unhappy at having nothing to report and was hoping to glimpse something within the last few minutes. I climbed the rubble of a demolished dwelling, its crumpled roof offering a good hiding place. Silently I cleared a space for myself and found that I had an extensive view over the town.

Before me was a street of plundered shops and a small *pension*. A small lorry and three American Willis jeeps bearing the Soviet star on the radiator turned the corner and drew up before the hotel. Soldiers jumped down from the vehicles, orders were given and small groups formed to explore the houses. My knees were trembling, but the Russians ignored my heap of ruins and concentrated on the standing buildings, all of which appeared abandoned. The Soviets began looting and had soon accumulated a substantial cache of fruit, vegetables and meat, a gramophone with records, candles, pictures and wine bottles. Since they had not been able to find spirits and other delicacies the mood became more aggressive and they embarked on an orgy of destruction. Furniture flew out of windows, books and clothes followed. The senior officer took over the most rewarding-looking building, the *pension*. I heard loud voices and glass breaking, then furniture being broken up. Suddenly there came a burst of MG-fire, loud orders and the anxious crying of a female. The Russians had apparently discovered the proprietor and his wife in hiding and kicked them both into the street at gunpoint. I estimated the man to be fifty, his wife thirty. Curious to see what happened next, the other groups returned to the vehicle. I counted twenty-three soldiers in all including the officer – a lieutenant. Something was discussed loudly, apparently in connection with the woman. The husband threw himself at the nearest of the soldiers, since he seemed to understand what the Soviets had in mind. A rifle butt was rammed into his back and he fell groaning to the ground. He was then lifted and bound to a lamppost by thirty turns of a long wire cable.

In the meantime the others had spreadeagled the woman across the hood of the jeep, two Red soldiers held one arm each, and two soldiers held one leg each. The officer drew his knife and to the accompaniment of amusing comments, which provoked much mirth from his contingent, cut away her stockings and lower clothing. From my hiding place about 30 metres away I had to look on while the woman was raped by all twenty-three soldiers. This took about an hour. I could not intervene, I was too close, could not hope to kill all of them and had no alternative hiding place.

A glance at my watch told me it was ten before nine, and in ten minutes my battalion would commence an artillery barrage of the town. Whether I could slip among my own men without them taking me for an infiltrator was an open question. At nine on the dot the artillery fired, but towards another suburb. To my surprise this did not appear to worry the Russians unduly, for they stowed their loot in their vehicles with no great haste, the unconscious woman still spread over the bonnet of the jeep.

Another dispute broke out with wild gesticulations centred on the young woman. Apparently agreement was reached, for while two of them held her legs apart, a third loaded a signal pistol with a flare and forced the muzzle into the woman's vagina. This appeared to present some difficulty, for she came to for a brief moment before the Russian soldier managed to pull the trigger. The flare entered her lower body and glowed furiously. I have never heard such a terrible cry in my life before or since as I heard at that instant. She was being burnt to death from within and her agony lasted for a minute or so. The Red soldiers shook hands, slapped each other on the back and began to climb aboard their vehicle. Just at that moment, about 200 metres off, I saw the advance party of my battalion making their way gingerly through the ruins of the village. If I opened fire now, I realized that I could probably hold out until the battalion closed in. I took careful aim and within a few seconds killed the officer and an NCO. The others were well-trained and went quickly to ground, returning a very precise fire that was too close for comfort, forcing me to cower low to avoid a hail of bullets. But I had succeeded in my objective. In dismay the Soviets saw the large number of German soldiers fanning out through the shadows and cover towards them and decided to take on the larger force. But they had a sniper at their backs and I knew where they were.

By some miracle the woman's husband survived the fire-fight unharmed. When we untied him he gazed in shock at his dead wife and twenty-two dead Russians. He seemed rooted to the spot, arms hanging at his sides. Suddenly he noticed that the twenty-third Russian was still alive, disarmed and immobile with a leg wound. With an awful cry the husband ran into the *pension* and emerged a few seconds later with a hatchet. The young Russian, a boy of no more than eighteen, watched in horror as the man approached. My sergeant held the man back while I made my report of the events of the preceding hour, then nodded and shrugged his shoulders.

The young Russian soldier was guilty of participating in gang rape and murder, either crime being punishable in the German *Wehrmacht* with death. Having been informed of his fate, the Red soldier was tied down and the husband allowed forward to carry out the sentence while we attended to other things. The hatchet swung to terrible screams and cries. Every bone in the Russian's body was cracked before his final dismemberment. Probably he had bled to death before the last act. Surveying the widely strewn body parts of the object of his hate, the man came to his senses and was at peace. Sobbing, he let drop the bloody hatchet and, falling to his knees, took the torso of his wife in his arms and held it close. After photographing the scene, we took up our weapons and left, not wishing to intrude in the man's inconsolable grief.

For the next two days in and around Nyiregyhaza we took on the 3rd Soviet Corps in house-to-house fighting. My allotted position was front line defence of battalion HQ. Russian mortar and artillery fire was laid with extraordinary precision in the vicinity of the command post. We heard a mortar salvo whispering over. Everybody dived for cover. I attempted to reach the nearby slit trench with a twisting roll but arrived a split-second late and caught part of the deafening explosion. Glowing metal splinters radiated outward in hundreds. A lucky turn of the head saved my life and the splinter missed killing me by a hair's breadth, ripping through the flesh of my forehead and touching the skull without splitting it. As if poleaxed I was thrown to the floor of the trench where I lay stunned for a few minutes. After I came to, I climbed out, streaming with blood, uncertain of how seriously I was wounded and calling in panic for a medic. Medical help was soon there, a stroke of good fortune that thousands of other wounded did not have. The medic inspected the injury and calmed me. It was only a flesh wound, the bone was undamaged. My legs were like jelly and the medic had to support me all the way to the dressing station. This time I had priority in the queue. A doctor cleaned and stitched the wound and I was given an hour to recover before reporting back for duty.

It was my third wound in action and on 27 October 1944 I received the Wound Badge in Silver. I reflected ironically that my three injuries had been mere trifles, but tens of thousands of others had paid for the deceptive silvery decoration with mutilation and lifelong pain.

Chapter 11

Partisans at the Saw-Mill:
I Win the Knights Cross

3.G.D. crossed the Theiss on 3 November 1944 and was integrated into the new front line. It was extremely cold and the river froze over. The accursed weather held up the Russian advance and helped us beat off whatever they threw at us, but we were so exhausted that no effective long-term resistance was possible, and by mid-November we had pulled back further to the industrial city of Miskolc.

After the fighting had been raging on their soil for several weeks, the political polarization of Hungary had become increasingly evident. The surrender and change of allegiance by entire Hungarian regiments tore holes in the front which could not be repaired, and created very dangerous problems for us. The fighting around Miskolc was always confused simply because it was impossible to know which way each particular Hungarian unit was facing at any one time: the fluidity was such as to render all military plans superfluous. Commanders led their units from the front in order to react at once to sudden emergencies.

In the field there were continuous rain and snow showers with temperatures down to ten degrees below freezing. With positions outside the city being little better than morass and swamp, saturated uniforms never dried. 3.G.D. faced seven Russian divisions and a mechanized corps, which in the conditions division believed could not be stopped. There was nothing for it but to withdraw into the city and fortify it. Here we were in a relatively strong position and held the centre although the Russians broke through the outskirts either side. Despite the catastrophe at Stalingrad, OKH still adhered to Hitler's instructions that 'fortress cities' must be held under all circumstances even though the original concept had envisaged air supply and eventual relief, neither of which the *Luftwaffe* was now capable of supplying. Accordingly, 'not giving an inch of ground'

118

meant the physical end of the troops involved. At Miskolc the 'fortress order' hung over the commanders' heads like the Sword of Damocles.

Since replacements could not be flown in, the loss of veteran command staff during the fighting had a wider dimension than would normally be the case, and losses were made good by temporary promotions. Thus companies might have a senior sergeant as commanding officer, and batteries a captain. Recently promoted to Major, Kloss was already battalion commander, but at Miskolc took over as commanding officer, G.J.R. 144.

On 10 November 1944 he summoned his battalion commanders to a situation conference at regimental HQ, the elegant villa of an industrialist. The installation of telephone communications was no longer possible in the chaos of continually changing front lines and command centres, and contact to division was by radio. This was problematic because the enemy could triangulate a fix on the transmitter and eliminate it with artillery. In the midst of battle it was naturally difficult to differentiate between ordinary salvoes of artillery and those aimed at a specific target, and this was the circumstance which made the situation conference a fateful one. Kloss was anxious to have the area beyond our perimeter reconnoitred, and for this reason I had been summoned to HQ. I was invited to make myself comfortable on a sofa in the smoking room, from where I watched the officers bent over their maps discussing the pros and cons of a counter-attack they had in mind. One could hear Russian shells detonating outside, but they did not sound very near.

The regimental radio car was parked in front of the villa transmitting a message to division when suddenly a Russian shell arrived and demolished the vehicle with a direct hit. The explosion shattered all the remaining windows of the villa, plaster flaked from the ceiling and splinters whizzed around the room. Everybody dropped to the floor except Major Kloss. He had been standing with his back to the window, and was hit on the back of the head. I saw his steel helmet fall over his forehead, then he toppled forward over the table and slipped to the ground. I jumped up and ran to his assistance. He was lying on his face and had a large open wound behind his right ear. As I turned him round he gave me a brief look of recognition before he died.

With the loss of Kloss I had been deprived not only of my guardian and benefactor, but a valued and esteemed friend. We buried him in the garden immediately, the grave marked by a fence post around which a cross in barbed wire had been fashioned, crowned by the steel helmet which in the decisive moment had not offered him the necessary protection.

I left regimental HQ and was reassigned to my original company. My commander was overjoyed to have a proven sniper on his staff and lent me out only grudgingly to battalion for special jobs. These loans had certain advantages, however, for I would be fed before leaving and then report myself unfed upon arrival at my destination, thus obtaining double rations. When changing location I went mainly at night aboard the horse-drawn provisions wagon, and if I knew the driver I could usually squeeze a third meal out of him.

On 1 December 1944, 3.G.D. abandoned the 'fortified citadel' of Miskolc and withdrew towards the Slovakian Erzgebirge mountains. The entire Eastern Front was in a state of collapse, and the *Wehrmacht* was embroiled in a war without fixed front lines, for besides the unstoppable tide of the Red Army we were now harried in the occupied territories by partisans and other irregulars. We no longer had a strategy: we were fighting to save our skins, to not fall prisoner to the Soviets or partisans, and to strive to reach the Reich again. The partisans were very difficult to combat since they operated to our rear and made surprise attacks from the depths of the hinterland. They had been developed into quasi-military organizations, often of battalion strength, with a strict command structure, often with Russian officers, and were well armed with Russian and German weapons. They were incorporated strategically into the operations of the Soviet forces, which coordinated their actions across the regions.

By the end of January 1945, the regiment had retreated to the Gran river running through the great valley between the Erzgebirge and Lower Tatra. Here 6.Army attempted to make strategic reformation of its forces to contain the Russian pressure along its sector of the front, and my regiment was sent on to the Waag Valley between the High and Lower Tatra ranges near the town of Rosenberg where, to our surprise, we received reinforcements. Among these were two snipers, green youngsters fresh from six wecks of basic training and four weeks' sniper school. The eighteen-year-olds had been exposed to ideological indoctrination along the way and were thirsting to be thrust to the front to help 'stem the Bolshevist advance' and where

120

they would reap 'a bloody harvest' with their sniper rifles. One of these two boys came to my battalion.

Partisan attacks were increasing in frequency and tenacity, and the regiment was embroiled in some very problematic situations because it was rarely possible to distinguish between partisan and civilian. The result was a further brutalization of the fighting. German soldiers who fell into partisan hands could expect to be mistreated and tortured to death. The *Jäger* took their revenge and all partisans rounded up were shot.

We took a very dim view of attacks on our supply wagons, for the desperately needed contents were not only a great loss to us, but would go towards strengthening the fighting ability of the partisans. Supply columns therefore came in for special protection and often had a sniper riding shotgun. One of the first duties of the new sniper was to accompany a five-horse wagon train outward bound to collect ammunition and provisions for the regiment. Near an apparently abandoned village, they were surprised by a band of partisans. A violent exchange of fire ensued in which the attackers were forced back into the village, where they concealed themselves in the dwelling houses. After surviving his baptism of fire, the young sniper proved himself a determined and well-drilled warrior and marksman. Under the guidance of a veteran *Obergefreiter* he succeeded in picking off a large number of partisans one after another in their hiding places. The German side captured the village putting the surviving partisans to flight. In clearing the area it was discovered that a number of the corpses were female. It could not be determined whether or not these were civilians since they wore no uniform or external distinguishing insignia. That they had no weapons was not a good guide since these would have been removed by the irregulars who had fled.

Two days later the young sniper was part of a patrol ambushed by partisans near a saw-mill. A bitter exchange of fire ensued in which the new boy lost contact with the group. He appears to have defended his position to the last bullet. The partisan band outnumbered the Germans and forced their withdrawal. The patrol saw the sniper raise his weapon above his head and surrender, and being led away to the usual kicks and beatings. They regained our lines and after receiving a brief report, the company commander decided on an immediate counter-attack in the hope of freeing the captive.

About an hour later our twenty-strong platoon approached the saw-mill where we observed that the partisans were still in occupancy.

After closing to within 50 metres, I opened the engagement by shooting dead the sentry. The partisans made a spirited fight of it but were soon aware that this was a battle-hardened enemy in greater numbers and so retreated from the saw-mill into an adjoining wood pursued by sixteen platoon members. Very soon I heard shooting.

I remained behind with three men and entered the building with them. It was filled with a strange humming noise in the background. We felt our way gingerly through the gloom. The leader entered the saw room, and tumbled out, white as chalk, a few seconds later. He was incapable of speech and could only stutter 'There! There!' and pointed inside. With weapons at the ready we entered. In the poor light we could make out that the humming noise came from the saw machinery. As our eyes accustomed to the darkness there gradually became visible a scene to make even the hardest, most brutalized soldier shudder.

On the saw table lay the torso of the young sniper. He had been sawn between the legs as far as the navel, and his arms and legs removed. To prevent his bleeding to death quickly, a torniquet of cord had been been applied to each limb before the sawing. Seized with fury, my three comrades dashed from the mill bent on revenge, but unfortunately for them the partisans had been overwhelmed and all put to death bar one who had slipped away unseen and was now about 350 metres away and crossing an open field towards thick woodland. Sitting on my right upturned ankle, I rested my left elbow on my upright left knee, adjusted the rifle strap around my shoulder and aimed the weapon. Two or three breaths, concentrate, hold the breath, shoot. A second later the fleeing partisan threw up his arms and fell forward. While one man went back into the mill to redeem the sniper's ID tags, I went to check on the partisan I had shot. With satisfaction I confirmed that my bullet, true between the shoulder blades, had taken his life mercifully.

There was no time to bury the young sniper, and to be quite honest I doubt if I had the stomach to collect up the body parts and scrape off the material adhering to the saw. We wanted to forget the scene as soon as possible. The company commander explained in the obligatory letter of consolation to the boy's family that during an action ahead of our lines, their son had received a bullet in the chest and had died a hero's death instantly. That was, we all agreed, the way it must have happened.

Our division pulled back further, crossed the border into Poland and dug in at Bielitz. Although Russian pressure was much less here – for the strongpoint of their offensive lay well to the south – we still had to face daily nuisance raids. My company held a sector of the front which ran along the edge of a village. The school and teacher's residence with cowstalls was incorporated into our front line. The Russians were 500 metres away across open country, the perfect field of fire for a sniper. The loft of the teacher's house recommended itself to me as a good observation position. I removed tiles from many places over the roof surface so that the enemy would not be able to identify my actual shooting position.

While engaged in these preparations, I thought I heard a child crying inside the house. I left my rifle and went downstairs with my 08 pistol drawn. I searched everywhere, including the cellar, but found nothing. In puzzlement, finally I entered the kitchen and while there heard muffled voices rising through the floorboards. I summoned two comrades to stand guard while I stamped on the trapdoor and shouted, 'Come out with your hands up!' In broken German the answer came at once, 'Don't shoot, here only mother and child.' The trapdoor opened and a woman of about forty emerged, followed by her seventy-year-old mother carrying a small child in her arms. She was the village schoolteacher living there with these two members of her family. She told me she wanted to stay, yet even when the great danger of the situation was explained to her she insisted on continuing to live in the house as long as German soldiers were there. One of the reasons for her refusal to leave was the presence of a cow which supplied fresh milk for her baby. This cow was a pitiful creature that stood all day, apathetic in its stall. It had been wounded in the belly by a shell splinter, and its intestines were bulging. Whenever the pain grew too great it would emit a long series of gurgled moos. It would have been a kindness to have put the animal out of its misery, but the milk was desperately needed for the baby. It was therefore agreed to make the best of it by having our men care for the cow while the women cooked and provided for us. The cowstall and teacher's house were connected by a deep trench: a hole in the corner wall of the cellar enabled the trench to be reached unseen.

I inhabited the loft for a couple of days, ears stuffed with cotton wool against the loud report of the rifle when I fired into the enemy positions. As expected, the Soviets soon identified my sniper-nest, and as their own sniper was hampered by distance and the inability to see through the roof, they called up a gun to finish me off. On the morning of the third day a lorry pulled up alongside a barn on their front line and an anti-tank gun was manhandled free. While three Russian soldiers fitted the gun with its various essential extras, others were transferring the ammunition from the lorry into the barn. The weather was calm and dry, the best conditions for sharpshooting. Since the purpose of the gun was to demolish a house within which a German sniper was hidden, I could not understand the carefree attitude with which the operation was handled by the Russians opposite. I had a good firm rest for the barrel and a comfortable seat. I took the first Russian working on the gun into my sights, aimed just above his head, and fired. The projectile hit him in the stomach and he folded like a jack-knife. Quickly I drew a bead on the second Russian. Bang, same result. They had to have been pretty raw recruits, for by now it should surely have occurred to them that they were under sniper fire, but no, the third man picked up the second in a fireman's lift. As he staggered towards the barn I shot him down. It had now dawned on the others that they were better off behind the house. To round off, it was more with speculation than serious intention that I decided to try to hit the aiming optic of the gun located through an aperture with sides twenty centimetres long in the splinter shield. I fired, but was not certain if I had been successful since I could see no evidence of damage visible through my field glasses, although the remaining Russians under cover were suddenly in a very athletic frame of mind and quickly vanished behind the house with the others. Soon the lorry's engine roared and the vehicle was driven off. The anti-tank gun, surrounded by its three dead crewmen, stood abandoned and forlorn. For the rest of the day the Russian lines were as if deserted. That evening battalion staff informed me that wireless monitoring had intercepted a message stating that the attempt with the anti-tank gun had been abandoned because the aiming optic had been shot up. I felt reason to be justifiably proud of my marksmanship.

Next day they sent my opposite number, a Soviet sniper who fired at anything that moved. His first victim was the old lady, shot in the chest as she left the trench near the cowstall. The explosive round tore her heart out. It would have been suicide to attempt to retrieve the body in daylight, and we had to place a guard on her daughter to stop her trying it. Eventually our remonstrations about leaving her son an orphan brought her to her senses. When darkness fell we buried the grandmother and over the next few days impressed upon the schoolteacher how important it was for her to remain out of sight. The Russians had learnt the same lesson and I did not find another target. The cow collapsed with her injury and could not stand unaided. The catering corps cook put the animal out of her misery with a pistol shot and the carcass ended up in the field kitchen.

A few days later divisional intelligence reported the 4.Ukrainian Army was preparing the decisive assault. 3.G.D. was put on maximum alert for Soviet surprise raids were probing our line for possible weak points. We packed and left for new positions, taking the schoolteacher and child along with us to the next town for safety.

On 2 March 1945 I was summoned to battalion HQ at Bielitz where an *Oberleutnant* of the regimental staff offered me his hand and said, 'My heartiest congratulations, it is my honour to award you the Führer's Sniper Badge in Gold', and taking my right arm attached the badge to my sleeve with a few token stitches. I received a simple photocopied typed certificate bearing the regimental stamp and signature of the regimental commander. Despite my understandable pride at receiving this award, it was a dangerous document to have in one's possession, and I went at once to the post room and mailed the certificate and the badge to my parents.

The *Wehrmacht* Sniper Badge is nowadays a rarity. Introduced at the end of 1944, it was awarded only rarely, since few snipers lived long enough to amass the number of kills required to earn it. A more elaborate certificate than a photocopied sheet of typing paper was not undertaken because of the lack of demand. Some recipients destroyed the badge for safety, and this has led to its rarity status.

National Socialist propaganda was tireless in its promises to produce a miracle weapon to turn the tide of war. The wish was there but the reality was not. The purpose of the bluff was to sharpen up the soldierly virtues towards self-sacrifice, and in this connection the sniper was an important role-player in the need to 'hold out'.[1]

I won my Iron Cross, First Class and the Knights Cross for my part in a single action on 2 April 1945 while attached to 8./144. One of our patrols had brought in a Russian prisoner who under interrogation volunteered information that a seventy-strong Soviet company of infantry was preparing to seize an unoccupied stretch of terrain 500 metres broad between two of our battalions. A platoon of eighteen veteran *Jäger* was hurriedly formed and given orders to locate the Soviet positions and delay the attack until the regiment could send reinforcements to seal the breach. It was also urgent to gain time for the evacuation of the wounded from a field hospital directly threatened by the Russians' line of advance. I was assigned to the platoon as flank and rearguard.

A soldier's chances of survival depend in no small degree on his feeling for what is possible. Here we were being asked to seek out and engage an infantry company that outnumbered us four-to-one and was occupying previously prepared positions, the locations of which we were not sure. I considered this to be a suicide mission and felt very bad about it. I went to the *Waffen und Geraet Offizier* or WuG (weapons and equipment officer) to exchange my Mauser carbine for a semi-automatic with optic and took another four magazines of explosive rounds with which I filled my tunic and trouser pockets. I then joined the others. That night an Opel Blitz lorry conveyed us to the endangered sector. We sat in the interior of the truck in silence, each man sunk in thought. We knew the dangers of what we faced. When the lorry stopped and the rear flap dropped down to signal the beginning of the mission, we leapt down, got our bearings, the platoon sergeant issued a few brief instructions and then led us off into the darkness.

I took up my position on the flank of the platoon to the rear, weapon at the ready. After an hour dawn began to show through the overcast sky to the east and we found ourselves ascending the gentle slope of a hillside. Suddenly a white star-shell hissed into the night sky and lit the area as bright as day. At the same time our ranks received the continuous rattle of murderous MG-fire. The platoon sergeant and six *Jäger* were hit, and fell to the ground groaning and writhing. Some of the eleven platoon survivors returned fire while five of the seven wounded were dragged out of sight into a shallow depression. The Russians now sprang up from their positions and attacked.

Apparently unnoticed I had thrown myself down some distance from the two wounded Germans remaining in the open, playing dead and hoping to gain for myself the element of surprise. I watched the first two waves of Soviets leave their dugouts, then arose zombie-like from the dead and began firing round after round of accurate fire over open sights at a range of about 80 metres. To be sure of the hit, and for the explosive round to do its work, I aimed for the area just above the hip. With devastating effect each bullet found its mark inside a Russian stomach, destroying a range of inner organs and intestines. The Soviets appeared stunned by having an unexpected apparition firing at them from an oblique angle on the flank, and then became visibly annoyed. Things were not going to plan for them. In the meantime my ten comrades had gathered their wits and were pouring towards the Russians a blistering fire. The magazine of my semi-automatic held ten rounds. Once the first clip was empty, every shot a hit, I swiftly fitted the second and continued firing. I could see the ground strewn with twenty or more Russian dead or writhing in terrible agony. After reloading with the third clip I became the target of a few desultory replies, but the awful screams of their wounded comrades had unsettled them so much that they aborted the attack and, apart from some withering fire in my direction, retired to their trench. I leapt up again and ran in wild zigzags to the two wounded *Jäger*, throwing myself down beside them in an unevenness in the ground which offered very little cover. So far I had come through the action without a scratch, but the dangerous sprint through the hail of bullets to render first aid to my wounded colleagues was of no avail. One was already dead and the platoon sergeant, whose torso had been raked by a machine-gun burst, died a few minutes later.

From their positions the Soviets were sweeping the foreground with small arms and light machine-gun fire, pinning me down with no hope of escape. The corpses of my two former colleagues were now useful as a bullet trap, while the sergeant's thigh made an excellent rest for my rifle barrel. While the remainder of the platoon gave me supporting fire from the background, my hour had now come. The Soviet positions consisted of two light MG nests at either end of a long trench. I had the inestimable advantage of facing an enemy who seemed to have no idea how dangerous a sniper could be even the distance of a football field away. Through the rifle scope I concentrated on the nearer nest, which was about 100 metres off. They knew where I was, of course, and while MG-fire spattered into the two cadavers, with my first two carefully aimed rounds I exploded the heads of the MG-gunner and his belt-feeder. There seemed to be no activity in the other nest, leaving the field clear for me to finish off the rest of them at leisure.

During a table talk at his headquarters on 25 September 1941, Hitler said that whereas he had nothing but admiration for the fighting spirit of the Russians, it was characterized by stupidity. How true that statement was, we were now about to discover. There were eighteen Russians in the long trench, and I could only see individuals within it if they stood up or moved incautiously at the parapet. Every so often a Russian would show his head and I would shoot his brains out. It was just like a shooting gallery at the local amusement park. When ten minutes had gone by, the trench was occupied by eighteen dead Russians, all of whom I had shot in the head. Finally the last machine-gun post came to life. The barrel of a weapon was thrown up on the parapet to fire a spray of bullets. The purpose of this seemed to be intended to cover the attempted flight of two Soviets, one of whom was injured and was being carried to safety piggy-back fashion. The MG-gunner showed me his head and received an explosive projectile which blasted it open. As he hurtled backwards he dragged his weapon down by the trigger, for a few seconds it pointed to the sky, and then the drum of the Degtyarov MG emptied in a long, harmless rattle.

The two fugitives had meanwhile proceeded some distance away from the trench. Now if I were carrying a wounded colleague piggy-back, and running in a straight line away from a sniper, I think I would want more protection to my rear than a knapsack of explosives. My projectile entered the knapsack carried on the back of the wounded Russian and both disappeared in the midst of a great flash and roar. Very possibly these same explosives would have been used to blow up our field hospital and, knowing the nature of the Soviets well by now, probably with the patients still in it.

The explosion was the final fanfare. Suddenly an eerie silence fell over the area. Even the cries of the Russian wounded had died away. After a few minutes the German infantry rose from their concealment and advanced with caution towards the enemy positions. Nothing stirred. Before us was a charnel ground upon which an entire Russian company had been wiped out to the last man. Over fifty dead littered the field, plus eighteen in the long trench and three machine-gunners. It was a scene reminiscent of medieval impressionistic art depicting hell.

The loss of their assault company had its pros and cons. The Russians overestimated our strength along this sector, revised their plan and regrouped. This gave us time to evacuate the field hospital which the Soviets considered to be of such vital military importance. On the debit side, however, they did not transfer their strongpoint elsewhere as hoped, but replaced the lost company with a much stronger contingent, and with a stiffening of snipers exacted bloody revenge for the massacre. We had dug-in temporarily to hold them at bay as ordered and received a sprinkling of reinforcements, but were so inadequately armed that no chance existed of overcoming the attack when it came the second time. With exceptional precision the snipers concentrated on senior NCOs and officers. Platoon Sergeant Willi Hohn stood up briefly to pass a hand signal to three stragglers when a conventional rifle bullet passed through his skull. His injury was so awful that an explosive bullet would have been kinder. I gave covering fire while four stout *Jäger* carried him away. He survived, but never recovered his sight, one of the many hundreds of thousands of blind or mutilated veterans who faced an uncertain future in the ruins of post-war Germany.

Rapidly interchanging my positions after each shot, I managed to score a few kills with my semi-automatic. When the assault came, fate smiled upon me kindly once more, and with the rearguard I managed to reach safety with seconds to spare.

A few days later I was summoned by the adjutant at regimental staff to attend battalion HQ. 'Herr *Obergefreiter*,' he beamed in greeting, 'you seem to be in the thick of it, don't you? First of all I have pride in awarding you the Iron Cross First Class for your brave exploit in the framework of the regiment's recent tactical mission and the evacuation of the field hospital. In confidence, what you did has attracted attention at the very highest divisional level. There is something else in the pipeline. Be prepared for a surprise.' He handed me an embellished scroll and a presentation case containing the order. I fastened the decoration at once to my left breast pocket, tossed the case into the mud upon leaving battalion HQ and mailed the certificate to my parents.

The highest award for bravery in the *Wehrmacht* was the German Cross in Gold, awarded to a serving soldier regardless of his rank. The commanding general, Army Group Centre, *Generalfeldmarschall* Schörner, was attempting, together with a regime of rigid discipline, to raise the troops' will to fight through the unorthodox award of decorations. Accordingly I was recommended for the Knights Cross, normally awarded only to officers and NCOs for personal bravery and outstanding contributions of strategic importance. The Knights Cross was one of the highest decorations of the *Wehrmacht* and its award was usually accompanied by a lavish celebration and a spot of home leave immediately after. Due to the collapse of the infrastructure, the value placed on the ceremony had tended to diminish of late, well-expressed in a droll mess-room cartoon, 'Kindly bring your cutlery when attending for medal awards', and the awards of the Knights Cross to Josef Roth and myself were similarly low key.

On Hitler's birthday, 20 April 1945, Josef and I were ordered to Corps HQ. An amphibious *Kübelwagen* was sent to fetch us and we alighted at Mönnighofen, a small village. Corps HQ was established in a kind of farmhouse, the activity resembling a beehive. Despatch riders and vehicles drew in and left; orders were barked; an abundance of staff officers were preoccupied with the impending evacuation. Our shabby uniforms and pinched, hardened faces must have made a very poor impression. A soldier brought us an opened can of herrings in tomato sauce, a chunk of bread and a pot of something tasty but indescribable. At least we had a full stomach while waiting, though, and that was something of a rarity in those days of impending disaster.

The hours went by. We had fallen asleep against a barn wall when a voice enquired loudly from within the HQ, 'Where are the gentlemen for the Knights Cross?' An NCO emerged and commented in a voice heavy with sarcasm, 'Are you the mountain troops to be knighted? Well kindly step this way, Herr *Oberst* has the sword ready for the ceremony.' We struggled to our feet and were led into a hallway where a colonel of the General Staff, his breeches bearing the red trouser stripe, approached carrying a file of papers. A soldier carrying a camera followed him. Josef and I, sniper rifles slung at the shoulder, came to attention.

'Stand easy, gentlemen,' the *Oberst* said jovially, 'please excuse the makeshift nature of this celebration. But I beg your understanding under the current circumstances. The Herr *Feldmarschall* was hoping to be present to congratulate you personally, but unfortunately there was no time. I will therefore proceed in his name.' At that he opened the file and read out:

Army Group Centre HQ, 20 April 1945.
To *Obergefreiter* Josef Allerberger!
I am greatly honoured to award you, on the Führer's instruction on the occasion of 20 April 1945, the Knights Cross of the Iron Cross and a gift hamper. From the reports of your commander I understand that you have provided repeated examples of outstanding military conduct and bravery. I wish you much luck and a safe homecoming.
Heil Hitler!
Generalfeldmarschall Schörner.

The same text was read out in respect of Josef Roth, after which the colonel gestured to a soldier to approach with a folded tent cloth bearing two Iron Crosses Second Class converted to Knights Crosses. The officer took up the first cross and ribbon, approached me, asked me if I had washed my neck. When I responded with a look of puzzlement he whispered, 'Just my little joke' and placed the decoration over my head to hang around my neck. After repeating the ceremony for Josef Roth, he said quietly, 'I am really proud to have soldiers like you in the Corps. My warmest congratulations and personal acknowledgement. I hope you survive in good health and return to the bosom of your families and your civilian life.' To camera flashes he shook my hand and explained, 'Once the general situation has stabilized, you will receive the proper Knights Cross medal with a scroll signed by the Führer. In the meantime I pass you this letter from the *Feldmarschall*. As a token of his personal esteem he encloses autographed photographs of himself and your divisional commander, General Klatt.'

A bitter undertone as he spoke was not lost on us. He knew we were only a fortnight or so away from capitulation. With a gesture of the hand he had our presentation hampers brought in, two wooden artillery chests of 100x50x30 centimetres filled with all manner of delicacies, and with a cheerful 'Best of luck, meine Herren!' the colonel left. A photographer asked me if I would pose briefly 'for the international Press' and steered me into the required position. A flash bulb flared twice and the sitting was over. Before he went I asked if he would send a print of each negative to my parents. He promised to do so, and kept his word. The ceremony concluded, my driver arrived for the chests and packed them aboard the *Kübelwagen* for the return journey. The hamper contents I shared out among comrades that same evening. From Corps HQ *Feldpost* I mailed the award documents home, but they never arrived, although the autographed photos of Schörner and Klatt mailed separately did make it.

Note:

1. In a long article published in the 1 October 1945 edition of the *Daily Telegraph*, Sir Roy Feddon, Special Technical Adviser to the UK Ministry of Aircraft Production, stated: 'I have seen enough of the Germans' design and production plans to realize that if they had managed to prolong the war some months longer, we would have been confronted with a set of entirely new and deadly developments in air warfare.'

The sentiment was repeated in a speech to the Society of Aeronautical Engineers by Lieutenant General Donald Leander Putt, deputy commanding general, USAAF Intelligence, Air Technical Service Command, in 1946, reported in *Harper's Magazine*, October 1946 edition, p. 329. Lieutenant General Putt stated that the Germans would probably have won the Second World War had the invasion been postponed by only six months. He was supported in this observation by US Navy Secretary James Forrestal in a statement to the *New York Times* on 28 August 1945: 'In general it may be said that the Germans were about six months too late in the development and mass production of new weapons.' The 'rocket surprise' for the world in general and England in particular to which Lieutenant General Putt alluded was undoubtedly the rocket/ramjet propelled Lippisch P-13 fighter-bomber, which was flown by the *Luftwaffe* at 2,440 km/hr on flight trials in January 1945 according to declassified Polish material (Kozakiewicz, *Bron rakietowa*, Glowny Instytut Mechaniki, 1951). The US archive has not released any information on the performance of the P-13 for any period after December 1944. The 'miracle bomb' of 'terrific destructive effect' was successfully tested at Ohrdruf in March 1945 and would have been mass-produced, and capable of being carried by a fighter. (Stevenson, *A Man Called Intrepid*, Sphere Books, p. 414: BIOS Final Report 142(g) 'Information from Targets of Interest in the Sonthofen Area', and 'DDR Judicial Enquiry of May 1962 into Wartime Events in the Ohrdruf Region', Arnstadt Municipal Archives).

Chapter 12

The Last Ditch:
Flying Courts and the Long Trudge Home

Our division had its back to the Reich border. By now the logistics, military communications and OKH command structure were in total disarray. In the effort to stave off defeat, Hitler Youth, men of pensionable age and untrained units were thrown into the fray, but had no hope of making an impression against an enemy present in overwhelming numbers on many fronts.

With the help of field-police and SS troops, 'flying courts' and seizure squads had been set up whose purpose was to uphold military discipline and fighting spirit. In tribunal hearings lasting only a few minutes, soldiers arrested for being absent from their units without valid papers were condemned as deserters and executed immediately. The defence that in the confusion of the front, military bureaucracy had collapsed was not acceptable. Many foreign volunteers and camp followers from the battle zones who had attached to individual units and followed their fortunes in defeat also met a violent and unjust end, and a large number were executed after trial by a flying court on alleged suspicion of subversion or collaboration with partisans. Although death was part of the daily routine for me, a case of the latter kind affected me greatly.

Coinciding with my arrival in the Ukraine in 1943, a young woman had attached herself to G.J.R. 144. Olga was twenty-two and became the paramour of an administrative officer. Apart from sharing his bed, she worked for the regimental staff as an interpreter. She was an uncomplicated, lusty blonde whose main aim was survival. She looked forward to the end of the war and a chance to settle somewhere in the West.

The identity of the person who denounced Olga as a partisan spy was never made known, although we had our private suspicions. I was present at her trial, which lasted ten minutes. The attempt by several NCOs and men to speak as witnesses on her behalf was refused with veiled references to their personal safety being in jeopardy if they persisted with their applications. The administrative officer did nothing to help his former lover. He was probably glad to be rid of her, for he was a married man and he would have been ruined if knowledge of the affair had reached home. After sentence, Olga was led out by several men in civilian clothing and made to stand on the flap of a lorry positioned below a tree. A length of telephone cable fashioned into a noose at one end was hung around her neck, the slack slung over a stout branch and secured. An SS man slapped the roof of the cab, the lorry moved forward, and Olga was left dangling. Death claimed her within a few minutes. The SS seemed to enjoy the theatre, but most *Jäger* turned away in disgust.

My regiment moved up to Mährisch-Ostrau. The Russians were at Brünn, although some of their troops were already in Berlin. The German Army – leaderless – fought on in isolated groups. In the east, endless streams of refugees headed westward, blocking the highways. 3.G.D. was one such group determined to resist and fight to the last. The end was close. It was an anachronism of the German death gasps that new weapons and equipment should suddenly arrive at the front. The battalion had mobilized for yet another relief attempt. I could hardly believe my eyes when a forty-strong *Waffen*-SS sniper company marched up. Over their uniforms they wore camouflage smocks with deep hoods, their helmets were fitted with a camouflaged cloth cover, and a special veil could be fitted to mask the face. Green webbing at the waist carried a Mauser K98k bayonet scabbard and a practical tool pack. Most had self-loading 43 rifles with 4-power scope, although two carried the new, fully automatic Sturmgewehr 44 with scope. The squad consisted of sixteen-year-old boys recruited only weeks previously. A two-week sniper course had transformed them into 'the fighting élite of the *Wehrmacht*', as they informed me. They were now fully prepared and determined to meet the enemy head on, convinced of their invincibility. Their leader was a *Sturmführer* (senior lieutenant) in his early twenties. To judge by his cold-blooded attitude, the survival of these boys came pretty low on his list of priorities. As I watched them march off to disappear without trace in the Russian fire dance, I could only think 'poor swine' – they looked to me like fodder for the saw-mill.

The division retreated to Olmütz in central Czechoslovakia. We were still fighting on 8 May 1945 when to our surprise the Russians ceased fire and returned to their positions. Aircraft dropped leaflets advising of the German capitulation and demanding that all *Wehrmacht* units lay down their arms and surrender. The divisional commander, General Klatt, was not prepared to do this because he feared for his men and had no guarantee what would become of them as captives. On the evening of the following day, a radio broadcast was made conveying the last order of the *Oberkommando der Wehrmacht* or OKW (The High Command of the *Wehrmacht*):

> [O]n the south east and east fronts, all principal unit staffs as far back as Dresden have been ordered to cease fire. The Czech insurrection over nearly all Bohemia and Moravia may hinder compliance with the terms of the capitulation and end communications in the region. The High Command has so far received no reports as to Army Groups Lohr, Rendulic and Schörner.

The full text of the message was read to our battalion by an officer. All knew now that they were confronted by an uncertain and possibly alarming future. General Klatt released all men of the division from their oath of allegiance so as to give each the vague possibility of reaching home by their own efforts rather than surrender. Wending one's way home was something easier said than done, for large numbers of Russian units had infiltrated to our rear through the great gaps in the front line and incited the Czech population to a bloodlust. Most of our men were in favour of attempting to reach the American forces on the Moldau river by obtaining lorry transport even though the roads were blocked by countless refugees. This seemed to me to offer a poor prospect of escaping Russian captivity. I decided to make for Austria on foot and in company with a friend, Peter Gollop. It would mean covering 250 kilometres through enemy territory, but I had sufficient experience to make my way cross-country unseen with no better aid than a compass. At all times the two of us would have to bear in mind the possibility of capture by Russian or Czech partisan forces, which might easily mean a very unpleasant death. To reduce this risk as much as possible we had to avoid any confrontation, and I elected to discard my sniper rifle in favour of a pistol and MP-40. To have carried a rifle with scope was suicidal. The fate meted out to persons identified as snipers was well-known. The weapon was only a piece of equipment, a means to an end, but all the same it was with a heavy heart that I decided it had to go. I located an SP-gun with a crowd of infantrymen aboard and begged a lift. I told the driver to wait an instant while I laid my rifle under the tracks. The vehicle moved forward and spewed out astern a small heap of crushed junk. With very few exceptions, all German snipers destroyed their weapons at the war's end or before being taken captive, and for that reason specimens of sniper rifles as war relics are very rare. A hand slapped my shoulder, making me start. I turned and looked into the eyes of the red-bearded Viking sergeant. 'Don't take it so tragically,' he counselled me, 'without it, your chances of reaching home safely are much improved. Enjoy the peace, if you make it.' Then he turned and disappeared into the undergrowth like a phantom.

Very few German units were prepared to surrender to the Soviets. Since most preferred to fight their way through to the West, the Soviets resumed the offensive on 10 May 1945 with massive tank and aerial attacks against the refugee columns, suspecting that many German soldiers would have inveigled themselves into the civilian ranks. Any small party of men was picked out and gunned by low-flying fighter aircraft. Peter Gollop and I resolved to move only by night, hiding up and sleeping by day.

On the second night, in the Sudetenland, we came upon an isolated farmhouse. It was occupied, for a flickering interior illumination could be seen through the windows. We were very hungry, and cherished hopes that we might be able to beg food from these peasants of German stock. We approached warily and tapped on a window pane. The curtain was pushed aside and a man's face appeared. He was holding a lighted candle and looked about fifty. Peering out, he saw us, unlatched the window and asked in very broken German what we wanted. I realized at once that he was a Czech and I stepped back instinctively into the shadows. At that time we knew nothing of the persecution and brutal deportation of the Sudeten Germans by the Czech population.

My inexperienced comrade threw caution to the wind and spoke up, offering a pair of new shoes in exchange for a meal. My distrust grew when I glimpsed on the wall of the room, a frame bearing a religious text in German and below it a German calendar for the year 1944. The Czech agreed to provide bread for the shoes and whispered suddenly, 'Russian soldier upstairs. Wait. I back in few minutes', and with that he withdrew.

Now I was even more uneasy. What was a Czech doing in a German house? Why was he sharing the house with a Russian soldier? I whispered to Peter, 'This stinks. Forget the shoes and let's get out of here', and pulled him away from the window by the sleeve of his uniform tunic.

'I don't think so,' he responded, and jerked his cuff free.

Heading for the small wood from which we had approached the house I called back insistently, 'Quick, get away from here, you idiot, before they nab you.' My determination unsettled him and, casting a final glance at the window, turned with some reluctance to join me. I was 30 metres away from the house and in darkness, Peter about 10 metres behind when the Czech reappeared at the window and opened fire with an MP-40. This galvanized Peter into action, and he sprinted towards me. At the first shot I had thrown myself to the ground and worked my own MP-40 into position. Seconds later, Peter was hit and fell face forward. Now I returned fire. Glass shattered and the wooden window frame splintered. I was not sure that I had hit the Czech, but at any rate he disappeared from sight and did not shoot again. Keeping low I reached Peter and dragged him by the collar as fast as I could into the wood, since I thought it likely that an armed party would soon emerge from the house. It remained as quiet as the grave, however. Once behind the cover of trees and vegetation I laid him flat on his stomach and examined his wounds. He was still alive but bleeding badly: I knew he would never survive these injuries, and he died a few minutes later.

I had been watching the farmhouse all the while from the corner of my eye. It was all quiet but I remained suspicious. Orienting myself by the pole star and my compass I set off at a trot. Alone, I had to be doubly watchful. To lure German soldiers from their hiding places, Czech partisans wore German uniforms. I knew about this ruse and hid myself from people in German uniform unless I was certain that they were bona fide.

At dawn on the second day following the farmhouse shooting I had heard muffled voices speaking in German. I stalked the group with great caution and while still concealed in undergrowth, identified them as being from my regiment's artillery battalion. In high tension at the precariousness of my situation, I called out a warning, rose from cover and was about to introduce myself when one of the gunners exclaimed: 'That is Josef Allerberger, the sniper with many kills, who has the gold Sniper Badge and the Knights Cross.' It was a twelve-strong group, led by *Oberfeldwebel* Viermeyer, a regimental warrant officer. As soon as my name was mentioned a heated discussion developed as to whether I should be allowed to join. The problem was that snipers had recently been made into hot properties by German propaganda and their faces, including mine, had been splashed all over the newspapers. It was therefore very probable that partisans and Russians alike knew my name and features by heart, and would be looking for me specifically among captives they took. Understandably, some of the group feared reprisals for themselves should their little band be captured and Josef Allerberger be found to have been travelling with it. This made me feel very uneasy, and I had just decided to continue alone when Viermeyer ended all discussion by offering me a place in their ranks provided I occupied the unfavoured rearguard position on the march. Thus I spent the next four days well behind the group, keeping to cover. The gunners were light-headed and confident at their chances of success. Each day they spent a little longer marching in daylight. On the fourth day they came across a dead Czech. He had been stabbed recently, for the blood on his clothing had not yet dried. In anxiety the group stood around the body discussing what best to do about it. Suddenly the corpse opened its eyes, sat up with a crazed look, spat blood, raised its MP-40 and pulled the trigger. The artillerists sprinted for cover and threw themselves to the ground. The entire magazine of bullets whistled harmlessly over their heads, and a few seconds later the Czech fell backwards and finally expired. The whole episode was bad news, for it was unlikely that this partisan was an independent.

Immediately after the incident, three German infantrymen stepped into the roadway about 50 metres ahead of the group shouting, 'Don't shoot, we are *Jäger* from Regiment 144, 3rd *Gebirgsdivision*.' From afar I recognized them as members of the regimental staff: the photographer, the sketch artist and an admin clerk called Schmidt, known as Schmidtle for short on account of his small stature. At my suggestion they were happy to fall in with me; as non-combatants they felt protected and somewhat safer. I felt the urge to distance myself from the gunners – their resentment of my presence was only too obvious. The photographer and Schmidtle each had a compass, and so I traded mine for half a tin of meat. Because of the strange incident of the dead Czech, both groups were anxious to move on as quickly as possible; group photos were taken and then we parted.

138

The four of us penetrated deep into the woods searching for a safe hiding place to spend the rest of the daylight. The artillerists had felt confident that it was safe to continue along the road by day, but that was their undoing, for barely half an hour had passed before we heard several furious bursts of MG-fire from quite close by. I took a compass bearing and went off to reconnoitre, keeping to dense bush. I had walked about a kilometre when I came to an open field where I saw the artillerists engaged in a violent fire-fight with a much larger group of Czech irregulars. Seven *Jägers* were strewn dead on the terrain. The whole situation looked very unfavourable for the five survivors and I decided that even if we four joined in we would merely be sacrificing our lives uselessly. Back at the hiding place I quickly briefed the others. By mutual agreement we destroyed our traces, broke camp and set off to find some other safe spot instead.

For days on end we walked by night and hid up by day, giving houses and villages a wide berth and avoiding open highways and footpaths. The artist had a nasty hand wound, received during a skirmish with Czech partisans. It had not been properly treated, and was badly inflamed. The man had a constant light fever and the wound, which had begun to stink, looked gangrenous. Whenever we came upon clear water we would clean it, wash the bandages and reapply them. We had nothing left to eat, and to keep us going chewed birch leaves and grass and drank water sweetened with saccharine from Schmidtle's small supply.

Day after day we plodded by night to the north-west, where lay the defeated Reich. We were fourteen days on the march. At dawn one morning we had just found a suitable hiding place on the banks of a clear stream and were tending the artist's wound when the sound of several lorries became audible. I left the others and went off to scout. After about 1,500 metres I found myself at a roadside. Four Mercedes lorries with SS markings were climbing a steep gradient in first gear. In the interiors I could make out tightly packed, unarmed German infantrymen. I ducked instinctively into the undergrowth, for I was very wary of SS units and the rough justice they dealt out. The war had been over for weeks of course, but we were still in an apparently German-controlled sector and the greatest caution was necessary, for as far as I knew it looked like the SS had not accepted the cessation of hostilities. Back at camp we calculated that we must be close to Reich territory. I reckoned that if we made 15 kilometres per night, twenty more days should see us home.

We had resumed our march for about an hour when we came across a farmhouse. A middle-aged lady was in the open arranging some garden implements. The photographer volunteered to address the lady on our behalf while we hid in the tall grass. Seconds later he beckoned us forward. 'We've done it, we're almost home,' he beamed, 'this place is 20 kilometres into Austria. The Americans have already been and gone, and Ivan is miles away.' The farmlady greeted us warmly and invited us into the house to share her meagre supply of food and to tend the artist's wound. She served us home-grown vegetables and potatoes, yoghurt and apple juice. After months of deprivation it tasted like the nectar of the gods, and we ate fit to burst. Next day we paid for our gluttony with diarrhoea. Like hundreds of thousands of mothers, she had lost her sons in the war. As she gave us their civilian clothes in exchange for our uniforms, tears rolled down her cheeks. We accepted her kindness in silence. Freshly showered, we lay in bed for the first time in months and slept deeply, stomachs filled and contented. After breakfasting we thanked the woman warmly and took our leave. Showing us the road to take, she waved until we were out of sight.

The brief sojourn had strengthened our resolve. Overconfident, we walked in daylight upon the open road after burying our weapons at the edge of a field, hoping for fair treatment from the Americans should we be captured. At midday we reached the hamlet which the farmlady had described. Chatting, we turned into the main street and froze in horror. Fifty metres ahead of us was a group of American soldiers and a large number of German prisoners. Wavering between flight and surrender, one of the GIs made our minds up for us. Unslinging his Garand self-loading sniper rifle he called out, 'Hands up, guys, don't move. War is over, Krauts, your bastard Hitler is dead. Your Scheiss-Führer can't help you any more. Come here, keep your hands up, move slowly.'

Although my knowledge of English was very basic, I realized it was best to do as he said. The American sniper would have shot us all dead within seconds if we had tried to run for it. Our war was now over – officially. Raising our hands, we approached the GIs slowly and received a superficial pat-down for weapons. I looked at the sniper rifle with interest. Technically it looked very solid and robust, but I was surprised that the scope was mounted so close to the line of sight.

A private pushed us among the other German prisoners. 'Sit down there,' he said with a cynical smile, 'and look forward to better times. I think you're really going to love your long holiday in Russia.' The word Russia ripped through me like a bullet.

The artist whispered, 'Shit, they're going to hand us over to Ivan. We've got to get out of here, or we've had it.' At that moment a US Army jeep leading two Mercedes lorries with SS markings and SS drivers pulled up alongside the prisoners, and those nearest had to climb aboard. As soon as the lorries were packed tight, they drove off smartly.

'Have a nice trip, you glorious Aryan heroes,' the GI called out.

Now I knew the significance of the SS lorries crammed with Germans which I had seen two days previously. They were deliveries to the Russians as fodder for the Gulags and lead mines. Our American guards were not very watchful since the prisoners were exhausted, and in no mood for escaping. The prisoners trusted the Americans and most did not believe that the US Army could play such a filthy trick on them.

The four of us were sitting on a waist-high wall, behind which was a bushy slope, a narrow valley bottom and then dense woodland, ideal cover for fugitives. With cautious whispers we agreed that we had to disappear as soon as possible before the next transports arrived. Three of us were bent on escape without any doubts, but Schmidtle hesitated, because he did not believe we would be handed over to the Russians. We agreed the order of disappearance: artist, photographer, Schmidtle and then me. The adrenalin was flowing in my veins, my heart beating furiously. We were risking our lives to survive. As three more transports drove into view, the first two men dropped over the wall unseen. When I told Schmidtle to jump, he refused. 'I've had enough of it,' he said, 'and I'm not risking my arse any more. Look, these guys are Americans. They simply wouldn't hand us over to Ivan.' The lorries were coming closer, time was short. Timing was everything, and the last moment had arrived.

'I'll wait for you thirty minutes at the edge of the wood,' I hissed, then rolled over the wall as the lorries squealed to a stop. Minutes later I joined the other two beyond the valley and told them what had transpired. Schmidtle never came. I saw him six years later, after he was released to the Federal Republic from the lead mines at Karaganda. He was by then a sick and broken man.

We three musketeers headed for Linz, moving by day but always alert to the possibility of American patrols. We had avoided a village and taken a footpath lined with thick vegetation on both sides when we were surprised by the cry of many voices. Fear ran through my bones as I saw a number of skeletal forms in striped suits running towards us, obviously intending to attack. They appeared pitifully emaciated and weak, and although easily outnumbering us it was child's play to fight them off with blows to the face and body. We had nothing worth stealing and realizing this they disengaged as rapidly as they had attacked. Breathlessly, we stared at one another in astonishment, and eventually concluded that they must have been homeless men who had escaped from a mental institution. Months later when we learnt that they were former inmates of a concentration camp who had escaped and were marauding through the district I felt justified in having defended myself, but the affair left a bad taste in the mouth.

Next day we reached Linz. This was where Hitler had spent his late childhood. The city seemed full of refugees. At the city gates we succeeded in finding a place aboard an Opel Blitz lorry, but after a few kilometres the journey ended at an American road block. Everybody had to get out and line up at the roadside. We were searched thoroughly and robbed of anything valuable or which might serve as a souvenir. On the instructions of an embittered NCO we had to remove our shirts and submit to an examination of the right armpit for the SS tattoo. Having survived that, we sat and waited. All day long, men of military age were held, searched, and then made to join our ranks. Towards evening we were about one hundred strong and loaded aboard lorries for Linz railway station where a train composed of a locomotive and countless cattle-trucks drew in. Its destination was a holding camp at Mauerkirchen. Tens of thousands of former *Wehrmacht* troops were forced to camp here in the open. It might have been deliberate, but the logistical problem had clearly defeated the Americans. Two days later they began to release the walking wounded. The artist's gangrenous hand needed proper medical treatment, and since the artist, the photographer and I all supposedly came from the same village, the artist was released into our custody as his carers. A discharge paper guaranteed us passage.

We were taken to Linz by lorry and unloaded at the railway station. We were free, our lives were again our own, even if it was difficult for the time being to grasp the fact. Our priority was to get

142

the artist to hospital, which we did at once. After taking leave of my two companions I waited for my connection to Salzburg. I watched a train roll out of the station, its passengers crammed aboard like sardines, some standing on the riding boards, others sitting on the carriage roofs. On the roof of the last car I espied the Viking. He recognized me at once and waved, then in a rare gesture for him raised his right hand to his peaked *Jäger* cap with its edelweiss badge, which to my astonishment he was still wearing, and gave me a final salute. I saluted back instinctively and then watched the train as it disappeared into the distance behind a cloud of smoke. I never saw the Viking again, but have never forgotten him.

I arrived home unannounced on 5 June 1945. My village slept as if knowledge of the great conflagration had escaped its attention. I had survived the inferno practically undamaged physically, although my heart was hard and scarred for life. The spirit of the war has never left me. The records show that I killed 257 Russians under the strict rules of calculating the tally. The actual number was inestimably greater. I was the second highest scoring *Wehrmacht* sniper after *Obergefreiter* Mathias Hetzenauer of Brixen near Kitzbühl, also attached to 3.G.D., with 345.

Was it right, what we did? Under the circumstances was there some alternative? These are questions to which a private soldier in the *Gebirgsjäger* can probably never find an answer. The simple infantryman never had a choice. It was simply a matter of fight, or die. We were soldiers, and we did our duty, and that was all there was to it.

Index